[IN MEMORY OF *Ken Radford*]

Published in 2008 by Stewart, Tabori & Chang
An imprint of Harry N. Abrams, Inc.

Library of Congress Cataloging-in-Publication Data

Radford, Leigh.
AlterKnits felt : imaginative projects for knitting and felting / by Leigh Radford ;
photography by John Mulligan.
p. cm.
"STC Craft/A Melanie Falick book."
Includes bibliographical references.
ISBN 978-1-58479-707-4 (alk. paper)
1. Knitting--Patterns. 2. Felting. I. Title.

TT825.R278 2008
746.43'2041--dc22
2008001972

Editor: Melanie Falick
Designer: Goodesign
Production Manager: Jacqueline Poirier

The text of this book was composed in Scala, Futura, and Fling.

Printed and bound in China
10 9 8 7 6 5 4 3 2 1

harry n. abrams, inc.
a subsidiary of La Martinière Groupe
115 West 18th Street
New York, NY 10011
www.hnabooks.com

AlterKNITS felt

Imaginative Projects FOR Knitting and Felting

LEIGH RADFORD

Photography by John Mulligan

STC CRAFT | A MELANIE FALICK BOOK | STEWART, TABORI & CHANG | NEW YORK

Create pleats after felting

Cut shape from top layer

Shibori bobbles

Felted bobbles

Pocket

leather handle

conte

introduction

— • —

Ever since my initial experience making felt, I'VE BEEN INTRIGUED BY ITS "MAGIC." MY FIRST PROJECT WAS A SMALL PINK ALPACA DRAWSTRING BAG THAT I KNITTED AND THEN FELTED BY HAND IN THE SINK. BY THE TIME I FINALLY FINISHED—IF I REMEMBER CORRECTLY THE FELTING TOOK OVER AN HOUR—MY ARMS WERE TIRED. BUT *I loved what I had created* AND THE PROCESS OF GETTING THERE.

TO THIS DAY, *this process still intrigues me.* I UNDERSTAND HOW FELTING HAPPENS AND THAT IT ISN'T REALLY MAGIC—WATER AND AGITATION CAUSE WOOL AND SOME OTHER ANIMAL FIBERS TO TWIST AROUND AND STICK TO ONE ANOTHER, THUS CLOSING UP THE "HOLES" IN THE FABRIC—BUT THERE STILL SEEMS TO BE SOMETHING MAGICAL ABOUT IT. I LOVE STARTING WITH A PIECE OF FABRIC THAT LOOKS AND FEELS A CERTAIN WAY *depending on my choice of yarn, gauge, and stitch pattern,* AND THEN FINISHING WITH A PIECE OF FABRIC THAT LOOKS AND FEELS COMPLETELY DIFFERENT. *I also love the flexibility of the felting process:* I CAN START WITH TWO IDENTICAL PIECES OF FABRIC AND THEN HANDLE THEM DIFFERENTLY DURING THE FELTING STAGE IN ORDER TO *alter the results.* FOR EXAMPLE, I MAY CHOOSE TO VARY THE AMOUNT OF TIME I FELT MY WORK, CHANGING THE DRAPE AND OVERALL FEEL, STRUCTURE, AND SIZE OF THE FINAL PIECE. OR I MAY CHOOSE TO FOLD OR PLEAT MY FABRIC AFTER IT'S FELTED IN ORDER TO *create a piece with a textured surface.*

WHEN I FIRST STARTED FELTING, *I sometimes found the results of my experiments frustrating.* RIGHT AWAY I NOTICED THAT MY WORK DID NOT SHRINK PROPORTIONATELY—FOR EXAMPLE, STOCKINETTE STITCH WOULD SHRINK TO ABOUT 65 PERCENT OF ITS ORIGINAL HEIGHT BUT ONLY 85 PERCENT OF ITS ORIGINAL WIDTH. I ALSO QUICKLY LEARNED THAT NOT ALL YARNS (OR STITCH PATTERNS) REACT THE SAME WAY WHEN FELTED, SO SOMETIMES WHEN I MADE WHAT I THOUGHT WAS A VERY SLIGHT MODIFICATION, *the result was drastically different.* REGARDLESS, I WAS HOOKED—*I wanted to felt everything.* I KNITTED HUMONGOUS STRIPED BAGS IN A MULTITUDE OF COLORS AND FELTED THEM TO MANAGEABLE SIZES. I STARTED COMBINING NOVELTY YARNS THAT I KNEW WOULDN'T FELT WITH WOOL YARN THAT I KNEW

FELTED WELL TO SEE HOW THE TWO WOULD WORK TOGETHER. I experimented with shibori techniques to create unusual textures. AS I TRIED OUT NEW IDEAS, I BECAME MORE AND MORE FASCINATED WITH THE RESULTS—BOTH THE SUCCESSES AND FAILURES—AND LEARNED SOMETHING NEW WITH EACH AND EVERY ENDEAVOR. I WAS PUSHING THE BOUNDARIES OF TRADITIONAL FELTING, EXPLORING different fibers, stitch patterns, shapes, and methods for texturizing, AND ENJOYING EVERY MINUTE OF IT.

AlterKnits Felt IS A COLLECTION OF THE PROJECTS I CONSIDER TO BE MY MOST SUCCESSFUL EXPLOR-ATIONS. IT INCLUDES PROJECTS made by knitting a fabric, then felting it, SOMETIMES APPLYING SPECIAL TECHNIQUES TO CREATE UNUSUAL SURFACE TEXTURES; TAKE A LOOK AT THE SHIBORI BOBBLE BAG ON PAGE 18, THE PLEATED CLOCHE ON PAGE 32, AND THE SHIBORI SCARF & CRAVAT ON PAGE 22. IT INCLUDES PROJECTS THAT REQUIRE RECYCLING PREEXISTING KNITS (FOR EXAMPLE, THRIFT-STORE SWEATERS), SUCH AS THE CAMP ROSE CUSHIONS ON PAGE 46 AND THE REVERSE APPLIQUE RUG ON PAGE 54. FINALLY, THERE ARE projects made from unspun fiber that is felted without ever being knitted, SUCH AS THE BALLS AND BUTTONS ON PAGE 90 AND THE FELTED RINGS ON PAGE 60. SOME OF THE PROJECTS ARE EASY AND QUICK, SUCH AS THE CIRCULAR COIN PURSES ON PAGE 26 AND SOME REQUIRE MORE OF A COMMITMENT, FOR EXAMPLE, THE CHRISTMAS TREE SKIRT ON PAGE 104.

I HAVE DONE MY BEST TO WRITE ALL OF THE PROJECT INSTRUCTIONS SO THAT YOU WILL BE ABLE TO DUPLICATE MY RESULTS, HOWEVER felting is an organic process that is affected by many variables, SUCH AS THE FIBERS USED, THE TYPE OF WATER YOU HAVE, AND HOW YOUR WASHING MACHINE OPERATES. I URGE YOU TO READ FELTING BASICS, WHICH STARTS ON PAGE 8, IN ORDER TO UNDERSTAND AND CONTROL WHAT YOU ARE DOING. ONCE YOU ARE FAMILIAR WITH THE BASICS, I also encourage you to experiment and explore, always staying engaged in the felting process SO THAT YOU CAN REACT TO WHAT IS ACTUALLY HAPPENING AND ALSO LEARN FROM EACH EXPERIENCE. ALONG THE WAY, I am sure you will discover your own tricks and innovative techniques, WHICH I'M HOPING YOU WILL SHARE WITH OTHERS. THAT WAY WE CAN ALL ENJOY TOGETHER THIS JOURNEY THROUGH THE ART OF FELTING.

Have Fun!

felting basics

— • —

IF YOU'VE EVER mistakenly thrown a wool sweater in a washing machine, YOU KNOW ABOUT FELT-ING—THE PROCESS BY WHICH CERTAIN ANIMAL FIBERS EXPOSED TO WATER AND AGITATION GRAB ONTO EACH OTHER TO create a dense, solid fabric. WHEN IT HAPPENS BY ACCIDENT, FELTING CAN BE RATHER DISTURBING. WHEN ACHIEVED ON PURPOSE, FELTING CAN BE BEAUTIFUL. This book is devoted to purposeful felting with beautiful results.

TECHNICALLY, THE TERM "FELTING" REFERS TO the process of making felt out of unspun fiber AND THE TERM "FULLING" REFERS TO THE PROCESS OF MAKING FELT OUT OF KNITTED OR WOVEN FABRIC. HOWEVER, THE TERM "FELTING" IS NOW COMMONLY USED FOR BOTH PROCESSES.

FELTING IS NOT AN EXACT SCIENCE. I HAVE TESTED AND RETESTED THE INSTRUCTIONS FOR ALL OF THE PROJECTS IN THIS BOOK, but to be sure you achieve successful results, you need to understand the following basic guidelines.

Fiber

Most but not all animal fibers will felt if exposed to moisture and agitation—in my experience, pure wool, alpaca, mohair, and llama all felt well. Some blends that include small percentages of fibers that don't felt on their own, such as silk or nylon, will also felt, although it may take a while.

When it comes to felting, all feltable fiber is not created equal. The speed at which, and the extent to which, a fiber will felt is affected by how the fiber was processed, including the chemicals it was exposed to during manufacturing and, if it is yarn, the way it was spun. Yarns that have been treated to make them machine-washable, often called superwash yarns, will not felt at all. Sometimes even certain colors of the same yarn will felt differently. It used to be that many chemically treated white yarns wouldn't felt at all, however these days that isn't as much of a problem. Still, I never skip the swatching step when I'm working with white or other very light-colored yarn for the first time.

Moisture

Moisture is vital to the felting process. As wool and other feltable fibers absorb moisture, their scales begin to swell and push open, helping the fibers to tangle. Although any type of moisture is likely to cause felting, for the projects in this book I stuck with water. The temperature of the water determines how fast your fabric will felt—typically the hotter the water, the faster the felting, which also means the less control you have over the process.

Shocking the fiber by alternating between hot and cold water will also speed up the felting process. However, changing the water temperature dramatically creates a rather dense, stiff fabric not suitable for many uses. Therefore, generally, I stick with hot water only when felting and cool or lukewarm water only when rinsing in order to be able to fine-tune my results.

Detergent

Although felting can be done with water alone, detergent helps to jump-start the process by causing the fibers' scales to swell and push outward and by changing the pH level of the water. It also softens the fibers so that the fabric produced isn't too coarse. Although any detergent will work, I generally use special wool washes like Eucalan or Soak.

During the felting process, you want to generate some lather, but not so much that your water is slippery to the touch. Too much detergent will slow down felting as it will cause fibers to slip over one another instead of tangle together.

Agitation

Generally, the more you agitate fiber, the quicker it will felt. Unspun fiber is typically agitated by hand by rubbing or massaging it. Knitted fiber can be felted by hand or in a machine; naturally, felting by hand takes significantly longer than felting by machine. To felt projects made with knitted fabric in this book, I ran them through one or more cycles in a washing machine. It's always important to check progress frequently when felting a project in the washing machine since felting is not reversible.

Estimating Shrinkage

Knitted fabric does not shrink proportionally when it is felted (that is to say, the length and width do not shrink equally). This is because stitches are not square. For example, when you are working in Stockinette stitch, each knit stitch is wider than it is tall and this affects the way fabric shrinks during felting. After years of felting, I have found that Stockinette stitch shrinks to approximately 85 percent of its original width and 65 percent of its original length. Every project is different, but I use this as a general guideline when I'm starting something new.

Felting Swatches

When working with a yarn I haven't felted before, I always begin by knitting two identical approximately 6 x 7" swatches in the stitch pattern I have planned for my project (basically, any size larger than 4" wide and tall is sufficient). If I don't know what stitch pattern I want to use at this point, I swatch in Stockinette stitch. Following is the process I use.

By creating two identical swatches, then felting one of them, I am able to estimate shrinkage of the finished project and get a sense of what the finished fabric will look and feel like.

1. Before felting, on a tag, record yarn name, fiber content, stitch and row gauge of swatches, and needle size used.

2. On both swatches, tie 2" long pieces of cotton yarn in a contrasting color at four points as follows (and shown above): one piece about 1" down from the top and one piece 4" down from there; one piece about ½" from the right side and one 4" to its left.

3. Felt one swatch (using the same method you will use for the final project, if possible), then air-dry.

4. On the felted swatch, measure the distance between the cotton ties for both length and height. Divide this measurement by 4" and you'll have the percentage of shrinkage. For example, if the width measurement between the cotton ties of the felted swatch measures 3⅜", divide this number by 4"—the original width between the cotton ties before it was felted—and you get .84 or 84 percent. If the height measurement between the cotton ties is 2⅝", divide this number by 4" and you get .65 or 65 percent. You now know that this yarn worked in Stockinette stitch on whatever needle size you used shrinks to approximately 84 percent of its original width and 65 percent of its original height.

5. Assess the results, considering how the fabric might be used. For example, if intended for a bag, is it sturdy and dense enough to withstand use? If it is for a scarf or something else you want to wear, how is it going to feel and drape over the body? Keeping these considerations in mind in the early stages of your work will help to ensure that you will be happy with your final results.

6. Tie the felted and unfelted swatches and the tag together. Store in a safe place so they can be referenced later.

I found that some laceweight yarns knitted at a loose gauge develop a wavy, irregular appearance when felted.

Felting in a Washing Machine

Felting can be done in a top-load, front-load, or portable washing machine. The process can take as little as 5 minutes or as long as 45 minutes, depending on the properties of the swatch or project, the action of the machine, and the desired result.

FELTING HANDKNITS IN TOP- AND FRONT-LOAD MACHINES: In my experience, front-load machines create softer pieces of felted fabric than top-load machines and take longer to complete the felting process. This is because the agitation cycle rotates more slowly in a front-load machine and is more gentle on your knitting. If you are using a front-load machine, check your manual to make sure you have an interrupt setting so that you can stop the machine to check the progress of your felting and then reset the wash cycle, as necessary. If your machine does not have an interrupt setting, you'll need to use a different machine.

Full Circle Purse (page 108)

1. Choose detergent and set washing machine to the following settings: hot water, lowest water level possible (you may not have a choice if you're using a front-load machine), highest agitation level possible

2. Fill the machine's tub with water. Add approximately 1 tablespoon of detergent.

3. Place your project into the machine and begin the wash cycle. *To speed up the felting process by increasing friction, include a pair of clean jeans, tennis shoes, or tennis balls with the project to be felted. Do not use bath towels! Towels create lint that will felt into your project.*

4. Approximately every 3 to 5 minutes, check on the felting progress by removing your project from the washing machine, gently squeezing it to remove excess moisture, and assessing how close it is to the desired size and texture. If necessary, return the project to the machine, resetting the wash cycle. Repeat this process until your project is felted as desired.

Your project is the most unstable at the beginning of the felting process. As you check on your work (especially at the beginning when it is still fairly loose and shapeless), make sure that pockets, handles, or other elements are not becoming tangled or sticking to each other in places where they are not meant to. If caught early enough, you can gently pull apart areas that have begun to felt together.

5. Once your project is felted to your satisfaction, remove it from the machine and rinse it in the sink with lukewarm to cool water. Roll project in a bath towel to remove excess water. Reshape project if necessary and air-dry on sweater rack. If you don't have a sweater rack, which allows air to circulate on all sides and speeds up the drying process, place project on a folded bath towel to dry.

Although some people run their felted work through the rinse cycle of the washing machine and/or in the dryer, I do not recommend either because these steps can create permanent creases and/or alter the finished shape of the project.

FELTING MACHINE-KNITS FROM THRIFT STORE IN WASHING MACHINE: For machine-knit sweaters and blankets that I pick up at thrift stores, I'm much more relaxed about the felting process. Since I didn't do the knitting and, in most cases, I can find a comparable item relatively easily if something goes wrong, I'm willing to take some risks. Here is my method.

Book & Laptop Sleeves (page 50)

1. Place thrift-store item into washing machine with same settings as given for handknits (see page 11). Run it through a complete wash and rinse cycle. Repeat the entire cycle until it is felted to desired thickness and size.

2. Place in dryer or set aside to air-dry. If needed, use a steam iron on the warm setting to smooth out creases or wrinkles in the felted fabric.

CLEAN UP AND CARE FOR YOUR WASHING MACHINE: The felting process causes fibers to come loose from your knitting as it felts. Left in your washing machine, these loose fibers can, over time, clog pipes or your machine. Putting your knitting in a standard-size zippered pillowcase or a net lingerie bag will help cut down on the amount of loose fibers left in your machine.

To prevent damage to a top-loader, after you have removed the felted project from the washing machine and while the drum is still full of water, dip a kitchen strainer through the water and remove as much excess fiber as possible (or put on dishwashing gloves and comb your hand through the water to gather fibers). Set your machine to drain and before the rinse cycle begins, wipe the sides of the drum with paper towels. If your drain hose empties into a utility basin, place a strainer under it to catch any additional fibers. When the rinse cycle is complete, wipe the drum again with paper towels, removing any additional fibers.

To prevent damage to a front loader, place a strainer under the drain hose before beginning the wash cycle.

PORTABLE WASHING MACHINES: I recently tried out a few portable washing machines and was really impressed with the Wonder Washer (see Sources for Supplies, page 132). This economical machine looks similar to a giant blender and can felt a knitting project that measures up to 14 x 14" in size. Here's the process I use.

1. To felt in the Wonder Washer, fill the bucket with hot water from the sink until the bucket is ½ to ⅔ full (you need enough water to submerge your project). Add about 6 to 8 cups of boiling water from a tea kettle to the water in the bucket. Do not pour the boiling water directly into an empty bucket.

2. Add approximately 2 teaspoons of detergent to the hot water, enough to generate suds but not so much that your water is slippery to the touch. If you need more detergent, add it in very small increments; if you realize you have added too much detergent, pour out some of the suds or add more water to dilute them.

3. Place your project into the bucket. Set the timer for 3 minutes and turn the machine on. After 3 minutes, transfer the partially felted piece from the water to a sink or extra pail. (You may want to put on a pair of dishwashing gloves to protect your hands from the hot water.) Squeeze the excess water from your work and check the felting progress. Return your work to the bucket, reset the timer,

and repeat this process. Since the bucket of the Wonder Washer is plastic, the water temperature will cool rather quickly. Check the water temperature, adding water from the tea kettle as needed.

4. Once your project is felted to your satisfaction, remove from the bucket and rinse with lukewarm to cool water in the sink. Roll project in a bath towel, removing excess water. Reshape project if necessary and air-dry on a sweater rack or on a folded, dry bath towel.

5. When felting is complete, pour the water in the bucket into your sink or bathtub using a sink strainer to prevent excess loose fibers from washing down your pipes.

Hand-Felting Knitted or Woven Fabric

Although you can also transform your knitting into felt by hand, it is a time-consuming and labor-intensive process, so I only recommend it for small projects.

To felt a project by hand, fill a basin with 2 to 3" of very hot water and add a teaspoon of detergent. Wearing dishwashing gloves to protect your hands, place your project in the water and scrunch and roll it around in the water. If you have something with a textured surface (such as a wash board, dish drain mat, bamboo sushi rolling mat, or even bubble wrap [as long as your water isn't hot enough to melt the plastic]), rub your project up against it to create friction and speed up the felting process. Change the direction of the rubbing and scrunching as you work and eventually, your knitting will begin to felt. Continue (prepare to be here a while—a small bag may take up to an hour to felt by hand) until work is completely felted and rinse.
Air-dry as explained on page 11 for machine-felted projects.

HAND-FELTING UNSPUN FIBER: I used unspun fiber to create the balls and buttons on page 90, and the pincushions on page 88. Instructions for hand-felting are included with those projects.

Felted Balls (page 90)

Needle Felting

Needle felting is the process of drawing or sculpting with unspun fiber. It is done by pressing a particular type of needle with a star-shaped point and barbed or notched shaft into the fiber in order to simultaneously grab, felt, and manipulate it. All of the needle felting in this book is done with clean, carded fiber, which—depending on the source—might be labeled as fleece, roving, or batt. Felting needles are available in a variety of sizes ranging from 32 to 42 gauge—the higher the gauge, the finer the needle and the finer the work you can do with it. A 36-gauge needle is a good all-purpose size and will work well for all of the projects in this book. You can also get a special tool that holds and allows you to felt with up to five felting needles at the same time (thus speeding up the process). Felting needles are fairly fragile—it's easy to break one (or more) as you figure out how much pressure you need to apply—so keep several on hand. To get started needle felting, you will also need hot, soapy water, a clean sponge, and a felting block, which is a foam block (usually about 4 x 6 x 2") that acts as a cushion to absorb the impact of the felting needle. I like using polystyrene foam blocks; regular foam rubber works as well but breaks down more quickly. Unspun fiber, felting blocks, and felting needles are all generally available at yarn and craft stores.

Needle Felting on Blue Jay Blanket (page 84)

NEEDLE FELTING ONTO KNIT OR WOVEN FABRIC: Place a plastic tablecloth or similar protective covering on your work surface. Place your fabric on top of your foam block, being careful not to stretch the fabric. Place within arm's reach a cup of very hot water mixed with two to three drops of soap. Place a small piece of roving (approximately 1" wide by 2" long) on top of your fabric where you want your design to be. Immerse a kitchen sponge in the hot water and drizzle the water onto the roving, or simply dip your fingers (with gloves on) into the water and pat the surface of the roving to dampen it. With the tip of your felting needle, gently poke and pull the roving repeatedly until it has begun to adhere to the fabric, adding additional roving, if needed, for desired coverage or shape. You don't need to use much force—a gentle, repetitive poking motion will felt your roving; if you apply too much pressure, your needle will break.

In the beginning stages of needle felting, if you decide you don't like the shape you've created, simply pull the partially felted roving free from your fabric and begin again. Later in the process, this isn't possible. Once you have completed your design, check the back of your work to make sure some of the fibers from your needle felting are showing through and are thus secured to the fabric. When you are satisfied with the coverage of your needle felting and feel it's securely felted to your fabric, set your work aside to air-dry.

CREATING NEEDLE-FELTED FABRIC: With this technique, you can form a flat piece of fabric or sculpt the roving into the desired shape. Place a section of roving on top of your foam block. Immerse a kitchen sponge in the hot water and drizzle the water onto the roving to dampen. With your felting needle, gently poke the roving repeatedly. Continue to poke roving until it has begun to felt or form a solid piece of fabric, adding additional roving, if needed, for desired coverage and thickness. You don't need to use much force—a gentle, repetitive poking motion will felt your roving.

Gently pull your roving up from the foam block occasionally as you work. The needle-felting process will punch the roving through to the foam and it will begin to stick. If you'd like to give your felt a cleaner edge, cut the edge with scissors; then, if desired, return the felt to your foam block and needle felt the cut edge until it is smooth and rounded. Once your felted fabric is the desired thickness and shape, set it aside to air-dry.

Felted Rings (page 60)

Rnd 5... ...d.

Rnd 13: [K1, (K1 F&b) twice, K15
(K1 F&b) twice, K1] twice.

Rnds: 14-21: Knit

Slip next 25 s...
or waste yar...
work first ...
in rows 2...

Row 22 (WS): ...

Rows 23-28: ...

Rows 29: K1
(K 2 tog) ...

Needle felt
design - pillow?

intarsia
project
palette

...1, (K1 F&b) twice,
...F&b) twice, K1] twice.
...if.
...(K1 F&b) twice, K15
...twice, K1] twice.
Knits: 14-21: Knit

Slip next 25 sts to st. hol...

projects

use your imagination →

shibori bobble bag

Shibori IS A JAPANESE TECHNIQUE FOR MANIPULATING FABRIC IN ORDER TO ALTER ITS SURFACE. FOR MY FIRST SHIBORI EXPERIMENT I SECURED BOTTLE CAPS IN knitted fabric with rubber bands, THEN FELTED IT. WHEN I REMOVED THE RUBBER BANDS AND BOTTLE CAPS (AFTER THE FABRIC WAS DRY), I SAW THAT THE FABRIC WHERE THEY HAD BEEN HAD NOT felted, WHEREAS THE OTHER AREAS OF THE FABRIC HAD. I loved the look BUT WANTED TO PUSH THIS IDEA A BIT FARTHER, SO I TRIED THE SAME PROCESS WITH ONE CHANGE: I removed the bottle caps midway THROUGH THE FELTING PROCESS CAUSING THE AREA WHERE THEY HAD BEEN TO FELT PARTIALLY. I LOVED THE texture and dimensionality of the result AND DECIDED TO USE THE SAME TECHNIQUE TO MAKE THIS BAG.

FINISHED MEASUREMENTS
26 x 20", before assembly
17½ x 15½", after felting, laid flat, including gussets
Results will depend on felting conditions and time spent felting.

YARN
Pear Tree Australia Summit (100% wool; 170 yards / 100 grams): 4 hanks summit white

NEEDLES
One 29" circular needle size US 9 (5.5 mm)
One 29" circular needle size US 11 (8 mm)
Change needle size if necessary to obtain the correct gauge.

NOTIONS
Stitch markers
Tapestry needle
10 large plastic bottle caps, 1½" diameter
20 medium plastic bottle caps, 1" diameter
20 small wooden beads, ½ to ⅝" diameter
50 small rubber bands (see Sources for Supplies, page 132)

Seam ripper or small pair of scissors, for cutting rubber bands
Two 22" leather handles with a 2" ring attached on each end (from Homestead Heirlooms—see Sources for Supplies, page 132)
Large-eye sewing needle and 1 yard fine linen or hemp yarn, for securely sewing felted tabs to handle rings

OPTIONAL: ½ yard fabric, fabric scissors, iron, dressmaker's pencil, and sewing machine, pins, needle, and thread, for lining
OPTIONAL: two ¾" magnetic closures

Note #1

Be creative when choosing objects to secure into the knitted fabric before felting! I used Odwalla juice caps, caps from pints of water, and wooden beads. You can use 1½" furniture "leg tips" or 1" PVC end caps from the hardware store, or anything else about the right size and shape.

GAUGE
13 sts and 18 rows = 4" (10 cm) in Stockinette stitch (St st) using larger needles

BAG

Using larger needles, CO 146 sts. Join for working in the rnd, being careful not to twist sts. Place marker (pm) at join and after 66th, 73rd, and 139th sts. Work even in St st for 3".

Increase 4 sts every 6 rnds 6 times as follows: Slip marker (sm) at beginning of rnd, M1, knit to next marker, M1, sm, knit to next marker, sm, M1, knit to next marker, M1, sm, knit to end of rnd—170 sts. Work even for 4", then shape bag as follows:

Decrease Rnd 1: [K21, ssk, k1, k2tog, k26, ssk, k1, k2tog, k21, knit 7 gusset sts] twice—162 sts.
Work 6 rnds even.

Decrease Rnd 2: [K21, ssk, k1, k2tog, k22, ssk, k1, k2tog, k21, knit 7 gusset sts] twice—154 sts.
Work 6 rnds even.

Decrease Rnd 3: [K21, ssk, k1, k2tog, k18, ssk, k1, k2tog, k21, knit 7 gusset sts] twice—146 sts.
Work 3 rnds even.

Decrease Rnd 4: [K21, ssk, k1, k2tog, k14, ssk, k1, k2tog, k21, knit 7 gusset sts] twice—138 sts.

Change to smaller needles and work even for 1½". Work 3 rnds Garter st as follows: purl 1 rnd, knit 1 rnd, purl 1 rnd. Next rnd, BO all sts except sts for 4 tabs, as follows: BO 12, knit 8 tab sts (including 1 st on right-hand needle), BO 22, knit 8 tab sts, BO 31, knit 8 tab sts, BO 22, knit 8 tab sts, BO 31 sts. Do *not* cut yarn.

TABS: With yarn still attached, work first set of 8 tab sts in St st until tab measures 4", then BO all 8 sts. Repeat for remaining tabs, joining in new lengths of yarn.

ASSEMBLY

With tapestry needle threaded with yarn, sew bottom seam. Turn bag inside out and flatten bottom. Sew a short seam across the triangular flap at each side approximately 3" from end of each triangle point, to form bottom and side gussets for bag, as shown in Step 1. Weave in loose ends. Turn bag RS out.

With RS of bag facing you, attach plastic bottle caps and wooden beads to one side of bag, leaving approximately 1 to 1½" between caps/beads, as follows: On WS, place each cap/bead at position shown in Step 2; on RS, wrap fabric around cap/bead, and secure by wrapping rubber band 2 or 3 times around fabric at base of cap/bead. Repeat for opposite side of bag.

FELTING

Begin felting, following instructions in Felting Basics on page 8. After 10 to 15 minutes, or when sts of the main body of the bag are partially felted, remove bag from machine and place in sink. Remove all caps and beads from bag by cutting rubber bands. Return bag to machine and continue felting until bag is fully felted.

Note #2

Removing the caps and beads from the partially felted bag will allow the fabric that was wrapped around them to felt, but will preserve the raised texture of the bobbles.

Once bag is fully felted, remove from machine. Rinse thoroughly with cool water, and roll bag in bath towel to remove excess water. Shape bag if necessary. If you would like to refine the shape of a bobble, reinsert a smaller cap or bead and secure with a rubber band. Lay bag flat to dry. Once bag is completely dry, cut any remaining rubber bands and remove caps and beads.

FINISHING

Fold first tab over ring at end of leather handle, and sew in place with linen or hemp yarn. Repeat for remaining tabs and rings.

LINING AND MAGNETIC CLOSURES *(optional)*
ASSEMBLE LINING: Cut fabric for 2 lining pieces and 1 pocket, as shown in Step 3. Fold pocket fabric under ¼" around all 4 sides and press with warm iron. Fold top of pocket under another ¼" and topstitch in place with sewing machine. Place WS of pocket on RS of one lining piece as shown in Step 4, and pin into place. Topstitch pocket into place, stitching approximately ⅛" from edge of pocket. With RS's together, machine-stitch 3 sides of lining pieces together. Working from the WS side of fabric, create bottom gusset by machine-sewing a horizontal seam 2¾" from corner as shown in Step 5. Turn lining RS out. Fold fabric around top of lining under approximately ½" and press with warm iron.

ATTACH MAGNETIC CLOSURES: With dressmaker's pencil, mark placement of magnetic closures on one side of lining as shown in Step 6, approximately 4" from side seams and 1¼" below top of lining. (Closures should line up under tabs, when lining is inserted into felted bag.) Using closures as guides, make ¼" cuts into fabric for closure prongs. On RS of fabric, insert closure prongs into cuts. On WS of fabric, slip flat disc (companion piece to closure half) over prongs. Press down on prongs, securing closure halves in place. Repeat with other halves of closures on opposite side of lining.

INSERT LINING: Turn lining WS out. Place lining into felted bag with WS of lining facing WS of bag. Pin lining into place. With sewing needle and thread, hand-sew lining to inside of felted bag.

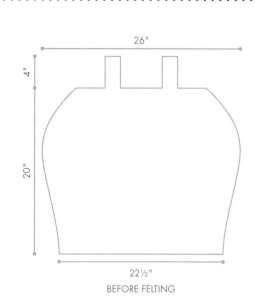

26"

4"

20"

22½"

BEFORE FELTING

SHIBORI BOBBLE BAG

STEP 1

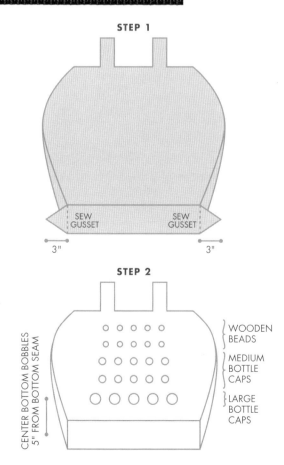

SEW GUSSET   SEW GUSSET

3"   3"

STEP 2

CENTER BOTTOM BOBBLES 5" FROM BOTTOM SEAM

WOODEN BEADS

MEDIUM BOTTLE CAPS

LARGE BOTTLE CAPS

STEP 3

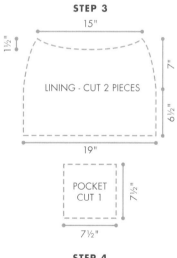

15"

1½"

7"

LINING - CUT 2 PIECES

6½"

19"

POCKET CUT 1

7½"

7½"

STEP 4

TOP STITCH

2½"

STEP 5

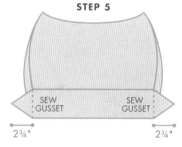

SEW GUSSET   SEW GUSSET

2¾"   2¾"

STEP 6

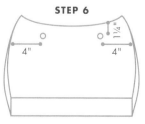

1¼"

4"   4"

- - - CUT
..... SEW
☐ RIGHT SIDE OF FABRIC
▨ WRONG SIDE OF FABRIC

shibori scarf & cravat

—— • ——

THIS luxurious alpaca piece, whether made in the shorter (cravat) length or longer (scarf) length, drapes beautifully AND FEELS FABULOUS AROUND THE NECK. TO CREATE THE UNUSUAL SURFACE DESIGN, YOU KNIT THE FABRIC, THEN wrap small sections of it with rubber bands, then felt it. WHEN THE felting process is complete and the fabric is dry, YOU REMOVE THE RUBBER BANDS TO reveal the newly texturized surface.

FINISHED MEASUREMENTS

CRAVAT:
9 x 51", before tying
9 x 43", after tying and before felting
4½ x 32¼", after felting

SCARF:
9 x 75", before tying
9 x 64", after tying and before felting
4½ x 43", after felting

Results will depend on felting conditions and time spent felting.

YARN

Blue Sky Alpacas Sport Weight (100% alpaca; 110 yards / 50 grams). Cravat: 2 hanks #519 amber, (MC), 2 yards #526 blue sky (CC). Scarf: 3 hanks (MC); shown in #73 tarnished gold

NEEDLES

One pair straight needles size US 10½ (6.5 mm)
Change needle size if necessary to obtain the correct gauge.

NOTIONS

Tapestry needle
50 to 100 small rubber bands (see Sources for Supplies, page 132)

Small lingerie bags with zippers
Seam ripper or small pair of scissors

GAUGE

15 sts and 20 rows = 4" (10 cm) in Stockinette stitch (St st)

CRAVAT AND SCARF

CO 34 sts.
Row 1 (RS): Knit.
Row 2: K2, purl to last 2 sts, k2.
Repeat Rows 1 and 2 until Cravat measures 51" and Scarf measures 75". BO all sts.

FINISHING

Weave in loose ends. Draw up approximately 1" square of your knitting and wrap rubber band around knit fabric 2 or 3 times to create bobble. Repeat, leaving approximately 1 to 2" between bobbles, until you have a 9" section of bobbles at one end of the Cravat and a 12" section of bobbles at each end of the Scarf, or as desired.

Note #1

The number of bobbles and the distance between them will determine the felted texture of your piece and its overall finished length. The more bobbles you create, the more knit fabric you are drawing up, thus creating a shorter finished piece.

CRAVAT EMBROIDERY

Thread CC on tapestry needle. Push needle up from WS of bobble to RS, leaving 1½" tail on WS of Cravat. Work French knot (see Special Techniques, page 129), wrapping yarn around needle 3 times and pushing the needle back down through bobble. Cut, leaving another 1½" tail. Repeat for desired number of bobbles. At Cravat end without bobbles, work three sections of satin stitch (see Special Techniques, page 129), each 1" wide and 3" long.

FELTING

Place each scarf into its own lingerie bag, to prevent tangling. Felt according to instructions in Felting Basics, page 8.

Note #2

Wearable pieces generally require less time to felt than a bag or other item where you want a more dense, sturdy fabric. Keep a close eye on the felting process, and stop felting while the scarves are still soft and have a nice drape.

While felted scarves are still wet, shape into final form by gently smoothing or stretching to desired shape. Lay flat or hang to dry; if you hang the scarves to dry, the weight of the water will concentrate at the bottom corners and pull the corners down, creating irregular curves at the bottom edges.

Once scarves are dry, cut rubber bands with seam ripper or scissors and remove. For Cravat, trim CC tails from French knots on WS.

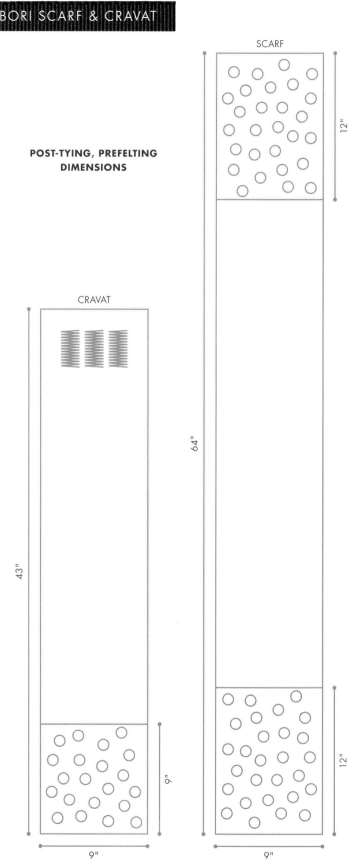

POST-TYING, PREFELTING DIMENSIONS

SCARF

12"

CRAVAT

64"

43"

9"

9"

12"

9"

circular coin purses

— • —

THESE coin purses are so easy and satisfying to make THAT EACH TIME I FINISHED ONE OF THE SAMPLES, I FOUND MYSELF PONDERING THE IDEA OF starting another in a new color. PLEASE don't be afraid of sewing in the zipper —BE PATIENT AND I GUARANTEE you'll be successful.

....

FINISHED MEASUREMENTS
6 ¼ x 9", before felting
5" diameter, after felting
Results will depend on felting conditions and time spent felting.

YARN
Brown Sheep Lamb's Pride Worsted (85% wool, 15% mohair; 190 yards / 113 grams): 1 skein. Shown in M102 orchid thistle, M83 raspberry, M151 chocolate souffle, M28 chianti

NEEDLES
One set of 3 double-pointed needles (dpn) size US 10 ½ (6.5 mm)
Change needle size if necessary to obtain the correct gauge.

NOTIONS
Stitch marker
Stitch holder or waste yarn
Tapestry needle
Smooth cotton waste yarn, for basting
7" zipper
Sewing pins, needle, and thread

GAUGE
16 sts and 19 rows = 4" (10 cm) in Stockinette stitch (St st)

BAG
CO 26 sts. Divide sts evenly on 2 dpns (13 sts per needle). Join for working in the rnd, being careful not to twist sts; place marker (pm) for beginning of rnd.

Note #1

Placing each half of the sts on one dpn and working with a third dpn makes it easy to keep track of the two sides of the bag, and to separate the two sides when creating the bag's opening. However, if you prefer, you can divide the sts among 3 or 4 dpns.

Rnds 1-2: Knit.
Rnd 3: [K1, (k1-f/b) twice, k7, (k1-f/b) twice, k1] twice—17 sts each needle.
Rnds 4-7: Knit.
Rnd 8: [K1, (k1-f/b) twice, k11, (k1-f/b) twice, k1] twice—21 sts each needle.
Rnds 9-12: Knit.
Rnd 13: [K1, (k1-f/b) twice, k15, (k1-f/b) twice, k1] twice—25 sts each needle.
Rnds 14-21: Knit.

Slip next 25 sts to st holder or waste yarn. Continuing in St st, work first side separately in rows as follows:

Row 22 (WS): Purl.
Rows 23-28: Work in St st.
Row 29: K1, [k2tog] twice, k15, [k2tog] twice, k1—21 sts.
Rows 30-33: Work in St st.
Row 34: P1, [p2tog] twice, p11, [p2tog] twice, p1—17 sts.

Rows 35-38: Work in St st.

Row 39: K1, [k2tog] twice, k7, [k2tog] twice, k1—13 sts.

Row 40: Purl.

Row 41: BO 2 sts, knit to end—11 sts.

Row 42: BO 2 sts, purl to end—9 sts.

BO all sts.

Slip sts for second side onto needles and work as for first side, beginning with Row 22.

FINISHING

With yarn threaded onto tapestry needle, sew bottom seam. Weave in loose ends.

FELTING

With cotton waste yarn threaded onto tapestry needle, loosely baste open portion of bag closed, leaving 2" tail at each end. Felt bag following instructions in Felting Basics, page 8.

Note #2

Loosely basting the opening closed keeps the opening from flaring during the felting process. Keep a very close eye on this section while felting—overfelting may cause it to felt together. If this area begins to felt together, gently pull the bag open.

ZIPPER

Once bag is completely dry, remove cotton basting thread by gently pulling on one end. Position zipper along open top of bag and pin into place. With sewing needle and thread, baste outer edge of zipper to bag from the WS; if necessary, cut opening wider or sew a portion of it closed, allowing zipper to fit into place. Turn bag RS out. Using invisible stitch (see Special Techniques, page 129), sew edge of bag to zipper.

CIRCULAR COIN PURSES

BEFORE FELTING

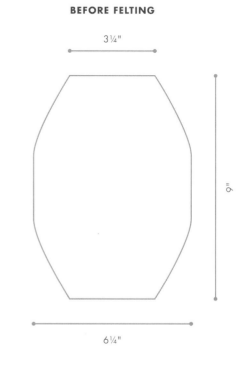

3¼"

9"

6¼"

circle & stripe bag

THIS *simple, contemporary* BAG IS AN ESPECIALLY GOOD ONE FOR *newbies to intarsia colorwork.* THE FELTING PROCESS MAGICALLY CLOSES UP AND HIDES ANY GAPS OR LOOSE AREAS IN THE KNITTING CAUSED BY *uneven tension at color changes* OR ANY OTHER MISHAPS.

FINISHED MEASUREMENTS
12½ x 45½", before assembly
10½ x 14¼", after felting
Results will depend on felting conditions and time spent felting.

YARN
Brown Sheep Lamb's Pride Worsted (85% wool, 15% mohair; 190 yards / 113 grams): 2 skeins M151 chocolate soufflé (A); 1 skein each M102 orchid thistle (B), M83 raspberry (C), M28 chianti (D), M105 pink (E)

NEEDLES
One pair straight needles size US 10½ (6.5 mm)
Change needle size if necessary to obtain the correct gauge.

NOTIONS
Stitch holder or waste yarn
Tapestry needle
Sewing needle
One 22" leather handle with tabs and linen lacing (from Heirloom Creations—see Sources for Supplies, page 132)

GAUGE
16 sts and 19 rows = 4" (10 cm) in Stockinette stitch (St st)

POCKET *(make 1)*
Using D, CO 27 sts. Work in St st for 10½". Slip sts onto st holder or waste yarn.

BAG

Using A, CO 50 sts. Working in St st, follow Rows 1-107 of large chart. Change to B and work for 2". Follow Rows 1-17 of small chart. Using B, continue in St st for 6¼", decreasing 1 st on first row and ending with a RS row—49 sts remain.

POCKET PLACEMENT: With WS facing, p11, BO center 27 sts, purl to end. Next row: Using D, k11, position pocket behind work and knit 27 pocket sts, k11.

Continuing in St st, work 2 more rows in D, then work the following stripe sequence 3 times: 3 rows E, 3C, 3A, 3B, 3D. Work 3 more rows in E, then 2 rows in C. Using C, BO all sts.

FINISHING

With WS of bag facing you, and using tapestry needle threaded with yarn, sew pocket into place using whip stitch, being careful that your seaming yarn does not show through to the RS of the fabric. Fold bag in half lengthwise and sew side seams.

FELTING

Felt bag following instructions in Felting Basics, page 8.

HANDLE

Once bag is completely dry, sew leather handle into place at side seams using provided leather tabs and linen lacing for thread.

CIRCLE & STRIPE BAG

	KNIT ON RS, PURL ON WS
	A
	B
	C
	D
	E

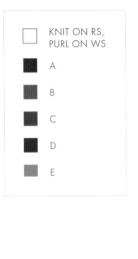

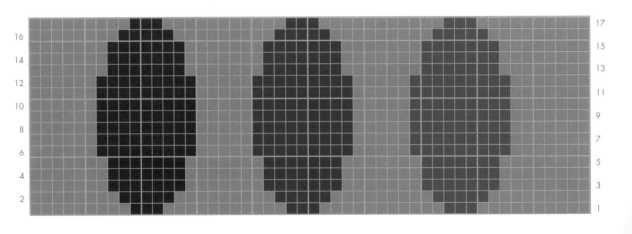

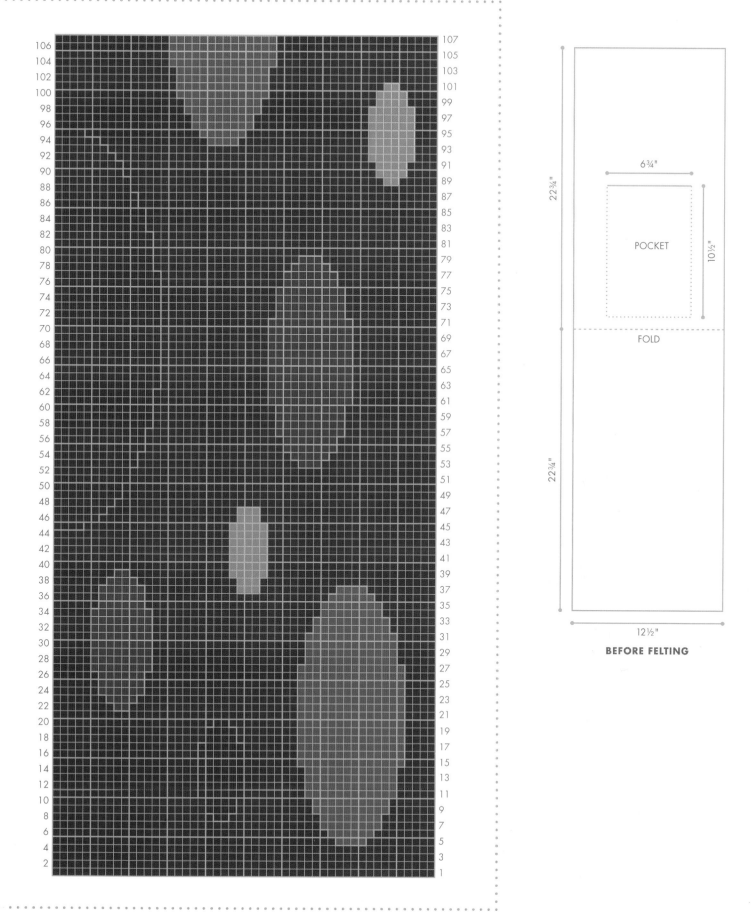

106   107
104   105
102   103
100   101
98   99
96   97
94   95
92   93
90   91
88   89
86   87
84   85
82   83
80   81
78   79
76   77
74   75
72   73
70   71
68   69
66   67
64   65
62   63
60   61
58   59
56   57
54   55
52   53
50   51
48   49
46   47
44   45
42   43
40   41
38   39
36   37
34   35
32   33
30   31
28   29
26   27
24   25
22   23
20   21
18   19
16   17
14   15
12   13
10   11
8   9
6   7
4   5
2   3
         1

22¾"

6¾"

POCKET

10½"

FOLD

22¾"

12½"

BEFORE FELTING

pleated cloche

THIS simple hat is molded into shape WHILE THE FABRIC IS WET, AND KEEPS ITS SHAPE ONCE IT IS DRY—A TACTILE PROCESS THAT REMINDS ME OF WORKING WITH CLAY.

FINISHED MEASUREMENTS

22 (24, 26)", before felting, around outside of hat
21 (23½, 25)", after felting, around outside of hat
Results will depend on felting conditions and time spent felting.

YARN

Vermont Organic Fiber Company O-Wool Classic (100% certified organic wool; 198 yards / 100 grams): 1 hank #8101 chocolate

NEEDLES

One 16" circular needle size US 11 (8 mm)
One set of 4 or 5 double-pointed needles (dpn) size US 11 (8 mm)
Change needle size if necessary to obtain the correct gauge.

NOTIONS

Stitch marker
Tapestry needle
Hat block, or bowl approximately the same circumference as your head and plastic bags or bubble wrap
Straight pins

GAUGE

12 sts and 18 rows = 4" (10 cm) in Stockinette stitch (St st)

HAT

Using circular needle, CO 66 (72, 78) sts. Join for working in the rnd, being careful not to twist sts; place marker (pm) for beginning of rnd. Purl 1 rnd, then knit 2 rnds. Work short rows (see Special Techniques, page 129) as follows:

Short Rows 1 and 2: K34 (36, 38), wrp-t, purl to 2 sts before marker, wrp-t.
Short Rows 3 and 4: K30 (32, 34), wrp-t, purl to 6 sts before marker, wrp-t.
Short Rows 5 and 6: K22 (24, 26), wrp-t, purl to 10 sts before marker, wrp-t.
Short Rows 7 and 8: K14 (16, 18), wrp-t, purl to 14 sts before marker, wrp-t.

Change to working in the rnd. Knit 1 rnd, working each wrap together with the st it wraps (see Special Techniques, page 129). Continue to work even in St st until work measures 11½ (12, 13)". Shape crown as follows, switching to dpns as necessary:

Rnd 1: *K4, k2tog; repeat from * to end—55 (60, 65) sts.
Rnds 2, 4, 6 and 8: Knit.
Rnd 3: *K3, k2tog; repeat from * to end—44 (48, 52) sts.
Rnd 5: *K2, k2tog; repeat from * to end—33 (36, 39) sts.
Rnd 7: *K1, k2tog; repeat from * to end—22 (24, 26) sts.
Rnd 9: *K2tog; repeat from * to end—11 (12, 13) sts.
Rnd 10: *K2tog; repeat from * to last 1 (0, 1) st, k1 (0, 1)—6 (6, 7) sts.

Cut yarn, leaving 4" tail. Using tapestry needle, thread tail through remaining sts. Pull tail snug and fasten off, weaving in loose ends on WS of hat.

Note

If small gaps remain at short-row turns, thread tapestry needle with yarn and tighten gaps, working from WS of fabric. Once hat is felted, your mending will not show.

FELTING

Felt hat following instructions in Felting Basics, page 8.

FINISHING

Shape felted hat over a hat form or an upside-down bowl. (You want the bowl to be approximately the circumference of your final size—if necessary, you can wrap a bowl with plastic bags or bubble wrap to get just the right size.) Beginning at the back of the hat, tuck the fabric into a 1" pleat. Continue to spiral both ends of the pleat around to the front of the hat, gradually decreasing its depth near the front of the hat. Angle the position of pleats as shown on page 32 or as desired. With straight pins, pin the pleats in place. Set the hat aside to dry.

Once the hat is completely dry (this may take several days), remove the straight pins.

pleated collar

THIS PIECE IS WORKED IN *Stockinette stitch with minimal shaping.* AFTER FELTING, WHILE THE *fabric is wet,* THE PLEATS ARE *secured with straight pins;* AFTER THE FABRIC IS DRY AND THE PINS ARE REMOVED, THE PLEATS REMAIN. *Really simple and really cool!*

FINISHED MEASUREMENTS

30 x 27¼", before felting

24½ x 16", after felting, unfolded

Results will depend on felting conditions and time spent felting.

YARN

Berroco Ultra Alpaca (50% alpaca, 50% wool; 215 yards / 100 grams): 2 hanks #6275 pea soup mix

NEEDLES

One 24" or 29" circular needle size US 10½ (6.5 mm)

Change needle size if necessary to obtain the correct gauge.

NOTIONS

Tapestry needle

9 small rubber bands (see Sources for Supplies, page 132)

Straight pins

4" Omnigrid scissors, or other small, very sharp scissors

Seam ripper

One button, any size

Sewing needle and thread

GAUGE

15 sts and 20 rows = 4" (10 cm) in Stockinette stitch (St st)

COLLAR

CO 86 sts. Increase as follows:

Row 1 (RS): K86, CO 4 sts—90 sts.

Row 2: P90, CO 4 sts—94 sts.

Row 3: [K1, M1] 4 times, knit to last 4 sts, [M1, k1] 4 times—102 sts.

Rows 4, 6, and 8: Purl.

Row 5: [K1, M1] 3 times, knit to last 3 sts, [M1, k1] 3 times—108 sts.

Row 7: [K1, M1] 2 times, knit to last 2 sts, [M1, k1] 2 times—112 sts.

Work short rows (see Special Techniques, page 129) as follows:

Row 9: Knit to last 12 sts, wrp-t.

Rows 10, 12, 14, 16, and 18: Purl to end.

Row 11: Knit to last 20 sts, wrp-t.

Row 13: Knit to last 28 sts, wrp-t.

Row 15: Knit to last 36 sts, wrp-t.

Row 17: Knit to last 44 sts, wrp-t.

Work even over all sts in St st for 20½", ending with a WS row. Decrease as follows:

Row 1 (RS): K1, [k2tog] twice, knit to last 5 sts, [k2tog] twice, k1—108 sts.

Rows 2, 4, and 6: Purl.

Row 3: K1, [k2tog] twice, knit to last 5 sts, [k2tog] twice, k1—104 sts.

Row 5: K1, [k2tog] 3 times, knit to last 7 sts, [k2tog] 3 times, k1—98 sts.

Row 7: K1, [k2tog] 4 times, knit to last 9 sts, [k2tog] 4 times, k1—90 sts.

BO all sts.

FINISHING

Weave in loose ends. Lay your fabric flat in front of you with RS up. Draw up or pinch approximately ½" square of your knitting and wrap rubber band around knit fabric 2 or 3 times to create bobble in upper left corner of fabric. Repeat, creating 9 bobbles (or desired number of bobbles); see Step 1 for bobble placement.

FELTING

Felt collar following instructions in Felting Basics, page 8.

Note

Wearable pieces generally require less time to felt than a bag or other item where you want a more dense, sturdy fabric. Keep a close eye on the felting process, and stop felting while the collar is still soft and has a nice drape.

POST-FELTING FINISHING

Lay wet, felted piece flat in front of you with RS up (felted bobbles should be in the upper left corner of your work). Create 5 pleats in upper right corner and pin in place with straight pins. (You may need to use several pins for each pleat.) See Step 2 for pleat length and placement.

Fold top 4½" of collar under. Create an additional pleat on underside of collar, as shown in Step 3. For best results, place collar around your own shoulders (while it is still wet), and work with the fabric by folding and tucking until you are pleased with the shape. Pin pleat in place.

Lay folded collar in front of you with bobbles on top. Create additional pleats on underside of collar and pin in place with straight pins, as shown in Step 4.

Allow folded and pleated collar to dry. Once collar is completely dry, remove straight pins from pleated areas and cut rubber bands from around bobbles using scissors or seam ripper. If desired, flatten bobbles with steam iron.

Using scissors, cut buttonhole through upper layer of left end of collar. Sew button to right end of collar.

☐ RIGHT SIDE OF FABRIC
▧ WRONG SIDE OF FABRIC

BEFORE FELTING

STEP 1

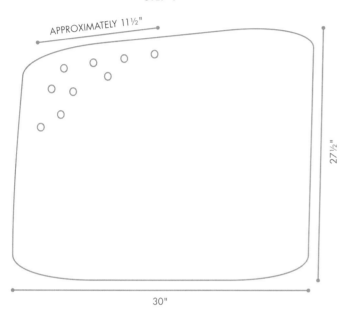

APPROXIMATELY 11½"

27½"

30"

AFTER FELTING

STEP 2

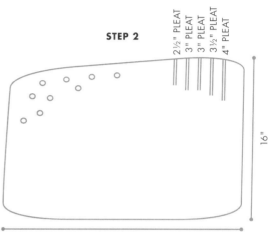

2½" PLEAT
3" PLEAT
3" PLEAT
3½" PLEAT
4" PLEAT

16"

24½"

STEP 3

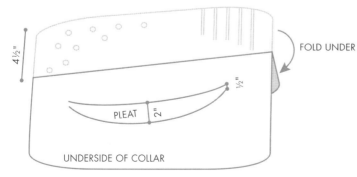

4½"

FOLD UNDER

½"

PLEAT   2"

UNDERSIDE OF COLLAR

STEP 4

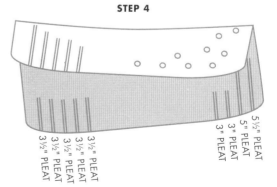

3½" PLEAT
3½" PLEAT
3½" PLEAT
3½" PLEAT
3½" PLEAT

3½" PLEAT
3" PLEAT
5" PLEAT
5½" PLEAT

simple zipper bag

—•—

SOMETIMES IT'S BEST TO *keep things simple*. AFTER SKETCHING THE DESIGN AND SHAPE FOR THIS BAG, I BEGAN TO THINK ABOUT HOW I WAS GOING TO *create the circular opening and handle*. I KNITTED AND FELTED SEVERAL SWATCHES, NONE OF WHICH PROVIDED ME WITH THE RIGHT SOLUTION. THEN I REALIZED THAT THE BEST WAY TO ACHIEVE THE SHAPING I WANTED WAS TO *simply cut the felted fabric*. A ZIPPER HAND-SEWN INTO THE *top opening provides a professional finish* AS WELL AS SOME EXTRA SECURITY.

....

FINISHED MEASUREMENTS
18¼ x 25½", before felting
12¼ x 16½", after felting
Results will depend on felting conditions and time
spent felting.

YARN
Manos del Uruguay Wool (100% wool; 135 yards / 100 grams):
2 hanks each #68 citric (A) and #26 rose (B)

NEEDLES
One pair straight needles size US 11 (8 mm)
Change needle size if necessary to obtain the correct gauge.

NOTIONS
Tapestry needle
Smooth cotton waste yarn, for basting
Quilter's pencil
Circle template, 4" in diameter (a glass or small bowl from
your kitchen works great)
4" Omnigrid scissors or other small, very sharp scissors
19" zipper
Sewing pins, needle, and thread

GAUGE
12 sts and 16 rows = 4" (10 cm) in Stockinette stitch (St st)

SIDE ONE
Using A, CO 55 sts. Work even in St st, slipping the first st of each row to create a chain selvedge, until piece measures 15" from CO edge, ending with a WS row.

Shaping Row 1 (RS): Slip 1, [ssk] twice, knit to end—2 fewer sts.
Work 5 rows even.
Repeat last 6 rows 3 times—47 sts.

Shaping Row 2: Slip 1, [ssk] twice, knit to last 5 sts, [k2tog] twice, k1—4 fewer sts.
Work 3 rows even.
Repeat last 4 rows once—39 sts.

Shaping Row 3: Slip 1, [ssk] 3 times, knit to last 5 sts, [k2tog] twice, k1—5 fewer sts.
Work 3 rows even.
Repeat last 4 rows once—29 sts.

Shaping Row 4: Slip 1, [ssk] 3 times, work to last 7 sts, [k2tog] 3 times, k1—6 fewer sts.
Work 3 rows even.
Work Shaping Row 4 once more—17 sts.

Purl one row.
BO 3 sts at beginning of next 2 rows—11 sts. BO all sts.

SIDE TWO

Using B, work as for Side One, reversing shaping.

ASSEMBLY

With yarn threaded onto tapestry needle, sew side and bottom seams as shown in Step 1. Turn bag WS out and flatten bottom as shown in Step 2. Sew a short seam across the triangular flap at each side approximately 2" from end of each triangle point, to form bottom and side gussets for bag. Weave in loose ends. Turn the bag RS out. With cotton waste yarn threaded onto tapestry needle, loosely baste open portion of bag closed, leaving 2" tail at each end.

Note

Loosely basting the opening closed keeps the opening from flaring during the felting process. Keep a very close eye on this section while felting—overfelting may cause it to felt together. If this area begins to felt together, gently pull the bag open.

FELTING

Felt bag following instructions in Felting Basics, page 8.

FINISHING

Once bag is completely dry, remove cotton basting thread by gently pulling on one end.

Using circle template and quilter's pencil, mark a 4" circle as shown in Step 3. Using scissors, cut a circle out of Side One. Repeat for Side Two.

Position zipper at opening and pin into place. With sewing needle and thread, baste outer edge of zipper to bag from the WS; if necessary, cut opening wider or sew a portion of it closed, allowing zipper to fit into place. Turn bag RS out. Using invisible stitch (see Special Techniques, page 129), sew edge of bag to zipper.

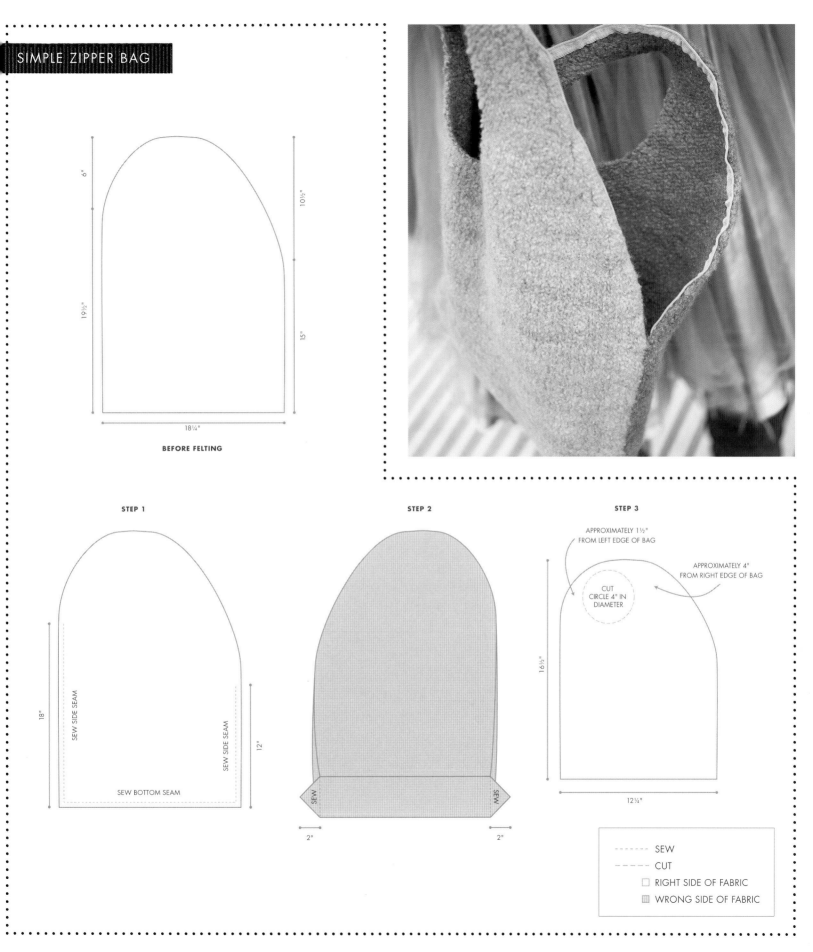

BEFORE FELTING

6"

10½"

19½"

15"

18¼"

STEP 1

18"

SEW SIDE SEAM

SEW SIDE SEAM

SEW BOTTOM SEAM

12"

STEP 2

SEW

SEW

2"

2"

STEP 3

APPROXIMATELY 1½" FROM LEFT EDGE OF BAG

APPROXIMATELY 4" FROM RIGHT EDGE OF BAG

CUT CIRCLE 4" IN DIAMETER

16½"

12¼"

- - - - - SEW
- - - - - CUT
☐ RIGHT SIDE OF FABRIC
▦ WRONG SIDE OF FABRIC

felted pillow with embroidery

—— • ——

THE green color OF THIS PILLOW WAS inspired by the colors in my backyard in the summer. THE embroidery design was inspired by some weeds I'VE GOT GROWING OUT THERE. THE ORGANIC WOOL YARN I CHOSE MAKES A VERY soft, smooth felted surface FOR EMBROIDERY——EASY TO WORK ON AND NOT TOO FURRY SO THE STITCHES AREN'T OBSCURED.

....

FINISHED MEASUREMENTS

22 x 52", before assembly
21½ x 24½", after assembly and before felting
18 x 18", after felting
Results will depend on felting conditions and time spent felting.

YARN

Vermont Organic Fiber Company O-Wool Classic
(100% certified organic wool; 198 yards / 100 grams):
2 hanks each #4302 willow (A) and #4303 evergreen (B)

NEEDLES

One pair straight needles size US 10 (6 mm)
Change needle size if necessary to obtain the correct gauge.

NOTIONS

Removable stitch markers
Straight pins
Tapestry needle
Smooth cotton waste yarn, for basting
Four 1" buttons
Sewing needle and thread
Embroidery needle
DMC cotton embroidery floss: 2 skeins #936, 1 skein #581
18 x 18" pillow form

GAUGE

14 sts and 21 rows = 4" (10 cm) in Stockinette stitch (St st)

LOWER PILLOW BACK

Using B, CO 72 sts. Work buttonholes as follows:
Row 1 (RS): K16, [BO 4, k8, (including 1 st on right-hand needle)] 3 times, BO 4, k16—56 sts.
Row 2: K16, [CO 3, k8] 3 times, CO 3, k16—68 sts.

Note #1

Binding off 4 sts for each buttonhole but casting on only 3 sts lets the buttonhole loops flare slightly.

Work 2 rows in Garter st. Change to St st and work even until piece measures 1½" from CO edge. Next RS row, increase 9 sts evenly across row—77 sts. Continue in St st until piece measures 16" from CO edge. Place removable st marker at beginning of row to indicate end of lower pillow back.

Note #2

To keep the opening at the pillow back from flaring, the stitch count is reduced slightly along the edges of the opening. Also, the opening is basted closed while felting.

PILLOW FRONT

Continue in St st until piece measures 22" from CO edge, ending with a WS row. Change to A and work even until piece measures 40½" from CO edge. Place another removable st marker at beginning of row to indicate end of pillow front.

UPPER PILLOW BACK

Continue in St st until work measures 51" from CO edge. Next RS row, decrease 9 sts evenly across row—68 sts. Change to Garter st and work 4 rows. BO all sts. Entire piece should measure 52".

ASSEMBLY

Fold pillow at markers, overlapping Lower Pillow Back over Upper Pillow Back by approximately 3", and pin into place; folded pillow will measure 24½" in length. With yarn threaded on a tapestry needle, sew side seams using mattress stitch (see Special Techniques, page 129), sewing through all three layers where Upper and Lower Pillow Backs overlap. Weave in loose ends. With cotton waste yarn threaded onto tapestry needle, loosely baste opening of pillow back closed, leaving 2" tail at each end.

Note #3

Loosely basting the opening closed keeps the opening from flaring during the felting process. Keep a very close eye on this section while felting—overfelting may cause it to felt together. If this area begins to felt together, gently pull the pillow open.

FELTING

Felt pillow following instructions in Felting Basics, page 8.

FINISHING

Once pillow is completely dry, remove cotton basting thread by gently pulling on one end. Sew buttons to Upper Pillow Back with sewing needle and thread. Thread embroidery needle with full strand of floss and embroider design as shown (see Special Techniques, page 129). Insert pillow form.

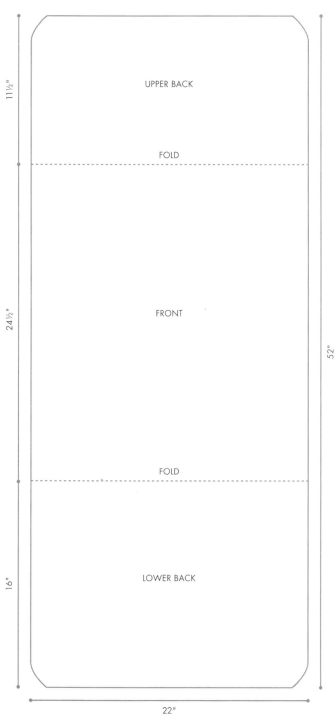

UPPER BACK

11½"

FOLD

24½"

FRONT

52"

FOLD

16"

LOWER BACK

22"

BEFORE FELTING

EMBROIDERY DESIGN

STEM STITCH

RUNNING STITCH

camp rose cushions & chair backs

WHEN I WAS GROWING UP, my *Aunt Jane* OWNED AND OPERATED a *riverside restaurant* CALLED *Camp Rose* IN AN *artsy area* OF NORTHERN CALIFORNIA. EVERY SUMMER MY FAMILY WOULD VISIT AUNT JANE FOR A COUPLE OF WEEKS, AND SHE WOULD ALWAYS TAKE US TO THE *local thrift stores* AND GARAGE SALES TO LOOK FOR *unique items that we could refurbish or reuse in artful ways.* JANE AND CAMP ROSE SERVED AS MY INSPIRATION FOR THESE CUSHIONS AND CHAIR BACKS, WHICH ARE MADE OUT OF RECYCLED SWEATERS AND THEIR OWN BLEND OF *old and new, traditional and contemporary.*

FINISHED MEASUREMENTS

CHAIR SEAT CUSHION:

15" wide across front edge
13¾" wide across back edge
15¾" deep from front to back

CHAIR BACK CUSHION:

16¼" wide across bottom opening
18" wide across top portion
10" deep from top to bottom

MATERIALS

6 large sweaters (100% wool—NOT machine washable):
3 sweaters per chair

NOTIONS

4" Omnigrid scissors or other small, very sharp scissors
2 Agne chairs from IKEA
1 sheet 36 x 55" butcher paper
Pencil
Ruler or yardstick
Sewing needle and thread
3 yards ³⁄₈" grosgrain ribbon, cut into eight 13½" pieces
(4 pieces per chair)
4 yards 12" wide Steam-A-Seam 2 double-sided fusible web
(2 yards per chair)

Steam iron
Straight pins
Sharp tapestry needle
8 yards sport-weight wool or linen yarn to match cushion color, such as Reynolds Soft Sea Wool or Louet Gems

Note #1

Each cushion is composed of three layers of felted fabric. Reverse appliqué designs are cut into the top layer, revealing the middle layer.

FELTING

Felt sweaters following instructions in Felting Basics, page 8.

Once sweaters are felted and dry, cut off sleeves and set aside. Cut along side and shoulder seams to separate sweater fronts and backs.

TEMPLATES

If creating cushions for Agne chairs from IKEA, simply enlarge the templates provided. If creating cushions for other chairs, create custom templates by tracing chair seat and chair back with pencil onto a piece of butcher paper.

CHAIR SEAT CUSHION *(make 2)*

Select 3 pieces of felted fabric to use for the 3 layers of your seat cushion. Using paper template for chair seat, cut each piece to seat shape. Using same template, cut 2 pieces of double-sided fusible web.

With sewing needle and thread, tack 4 pieces of ribbon to middle layer of cushion, as shown on template, for use as ties.

Remove paper backing from one side of first piece of fusible web and stick to WS of top layer. Following directions provided with fusible web, iron to fuse top layer and fusible web. Let cool. Pin paper template to RS of top layer. Using scissors, cut out ginko or circle design, being sure to cut through both felted fabric and fusible web.

Note # 2

Initially fusing the fusible web to the top layer only (and not to the top and middle layers simultaneously) makes it easier to cut the ginko or circle design precisely.

Remove paper backing from other side of first piece of fusible web and stick to middle layer of cushion. Iron to fuse top and middle layers, being careful to keep ribbon ties free. Let cool.

Remove paper backings from second piece of fusible web, and stick to middle and bottom layers. With bottom layer face up, iron to fuse middle and bottom layers. Let cool.

With sharp tapestry needle and sport-weight yarn, work running st around perimeter of cushion as shown on template.

CHAIR BACK CUSHION *(make 2)*

Using paper template for chair back, cut 3 layers of felted fabric and 1 layer of fusible web. Fuse first 2 layers as for seat cushion (omitting ribbon ties) and cut out design as for chair seat cushion. Pin third layer to WS of middle layer. With sharp tapestry needle and sport-weight yarn, sew third layer to first 2 layers with running st, leaving bottom edge open, as shown on template.

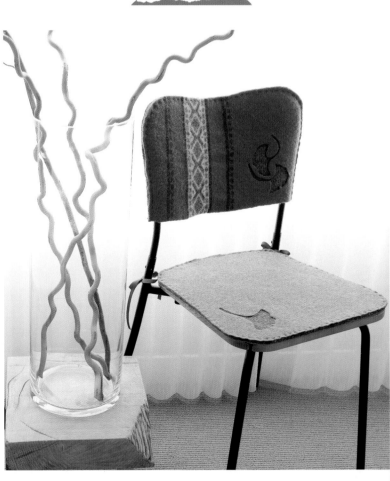

- - - RUNNING STITCH

CHAIR SEAT TEMPLATES

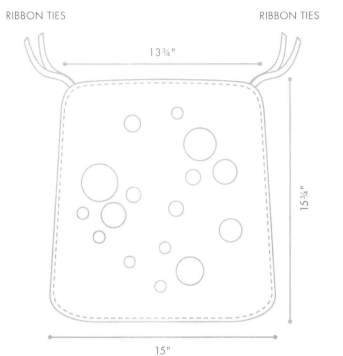

RIBBON TIES

RIBBON TIES

13¾"

15¾"

15"

RIBBON TIES

RIBBON TIES

13¾"

15¾"

15"

CHAIR BACK TEMPLATES

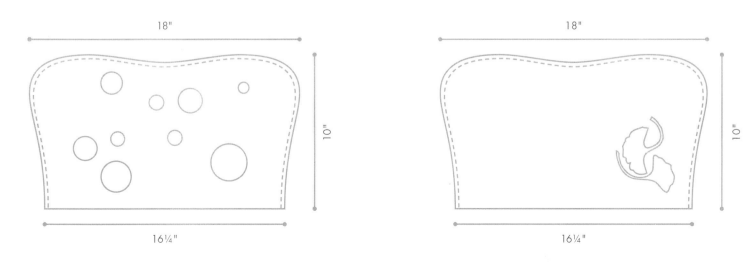

18"

10"

16¼"

18"

10"

16¼"

book & laptop sleeves

EVER SINCE I recycled my first sweaters—FOR A BLANKET PROJECT IN MY FIRST BOOK AlterKnits— I'VE BEEN KEEN TO FIND NOVEL WAYS TO give old sweaters new life. FOR THIS PROJECT I transformed thrift-shop sweaters into sleeves THAT CAN BE USED TO protect a laptop or a special book. I FIND THEM ESPECIALLY USEFUL WHEN I'M TRAVELING AND MY belongings are subject to extra jostling.

FINISHED MEASUREMENTS

LAPTOP SLEEVE:
14" wide
10½" tall
1½" deep

BOOK SLEEVE:
11" wide
9½" tall
1¼" deep

MATERIALS

1 large sweater for each laptop or book sleeve
(100% wool—NOT machine washable)

NOTIONS

Fabric scissors
Butcher paper
Pencil
Ruler or yardstick
Straight pins
Sharp tapestry needle and 2 yards sport-weight wool or linen yarn, or sewing machine and sewing thread

Note

You can sew these sleeves by hand or by machine, depending on the thickness of the felted fabric. I chose to hand-sew the laptop sleeve at left with a running stitch because the fabric was so thick. I machine-sewed the book sleeve on page 52 with a straight stitch.

FELTING

Felt sweaters following instructions in Felting Basics, page 8.

Once sweaters are felted and dry, cut off sleeves and set aside. Cut along side and shoulder seams to separate sweater fronts and backs.

LAPTOP SLEEVE

Cut the following templates from butcher paper:
14½ x 10¾", for front and back
2 x 10¾", for side gussets
2 x 14½", for bottom gusset

Pin butcher-paper templates to felted fabric, positioning templates to incorporate sweater design or motifs as desired. Cut 1 front, 1 back, 2 side gussets, and 1 bottom gusset.

With WS's together, align side edges of front and first side gusset. Sew together, using ¼" seam allowance, stopping ¼" from bottom edge. Repeat with second side gusset. Sew back to side gussets, as shown in Step 1.

With WS's together, pin bottom gusset in place. Sew, using ¼" seam allowance, beginning and ending seams ¼" from fabric edges, as shown in Step 2.

BOOK SLEEVE

Work as for laptop sleeve, using paper templates in the following sizes:

11½ x 9¾", for front and back
1¾ x 9¾", for side gussets
1¾ x 11½", for bottom gusset

CUSTOM SLEEVES

To create a sleeve in a custom size, simply trace the shape you would like to create onto butcher paper, adding ¼" seam allowances to sides and bottom of sleeve.

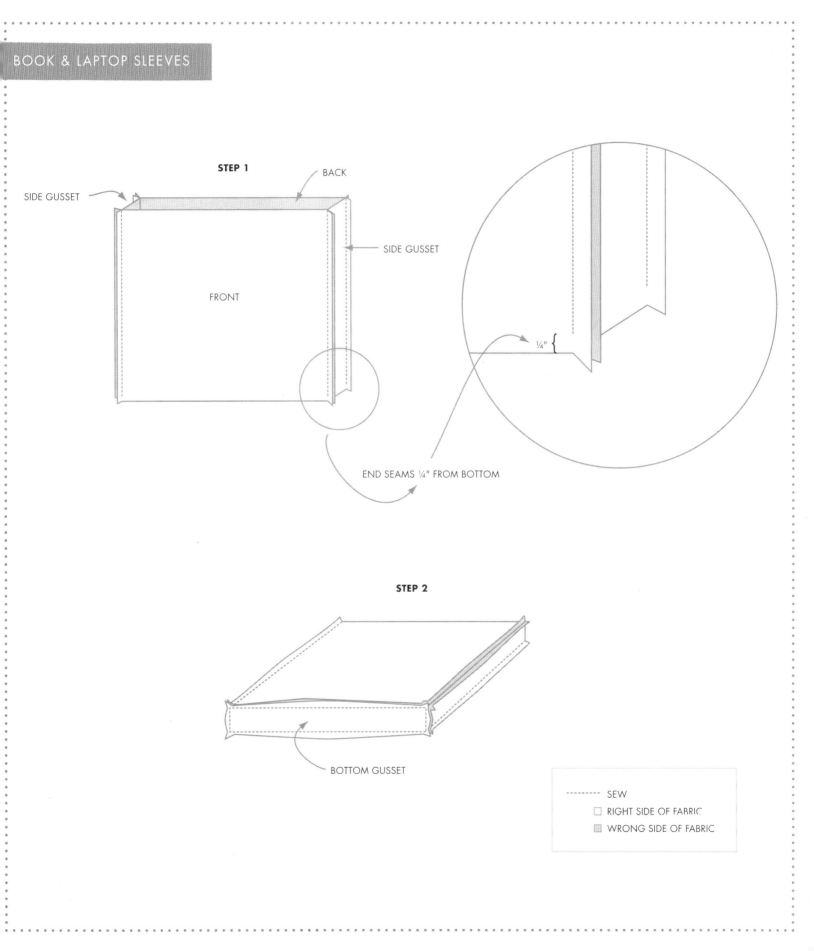

STEP 1

SIDE GUSSET

BACK

SIDE GUSSET

FRONT

¼"

END SEAMS ¼" FROM BOTTOM

STEP 2

BOTTOM GUSSET

---------- SEW
☐ RIGHT SIDE OF FABRIC
▨ WRONG SIDE OF FABRIC

reverse appliqué rug

DURING MY FREQUENT *forays into thrift stores* IN SEARCH OF WOOL SWEATERS TO FELT FOR PROJECTS FOR THIS BOOK, I OCCASIONALLY CAME ACROSS *wool blankets* I COULDN'T RESIST BUYING. AT HOME I CAME UP WITH THE IDEA OF *recreating them as rugs.*

FINISHED MEASUREMENTS
36 x 54"

MATERIALS
2 wool blankets (NOT machine-washable)

NOTIONS
Fabric scissors
Straight pins
4" Omnigrid scissors or other small, very sharp scissors
Sharp tapestry needle
20 to 25 yards sport-weight wool or linen yarn to match blanket color

FELTING
Felt blankets following instructions in Felting Basics, page 8.

RUG
Once blankets are dry, use fabric scissors to cut each to measure 36 x 54".

Copy the cutting template and enlarge 564%.

Note #1

A full-scale PDF of the template, which can be printed out full-size at a copy shop, is available at leighradford.com.

Position the template on the lower portion of the top blanket, with the design 3½" from the bottom edge and 1" from the right and left edges. Pin template into place, with straight pins all around the design, to keep it secure while cutting.

Note #2

The tan blanket I chose for the top layer had a red stripe across the top. I chose to feature the stripe on my blanket and cut my top layer so that the stripe ran horizontally across its top. Had I wanted the entire top layer to be tan, I could have cut the blanket so that the stripe was not part of this design.

With scissors, cut design as indicated, being sure to cut through paper template and wool blanket. Once entire design is cut, remove pins and paper template.

Place top blanket with cut design on top of bottom blanket, with WS of top blanket against RS of bottom blanket. Pin layers together. With sharp tapestry needle threaded with yarn, work running stitch around reverse appliqué design. Work blanket stitch around perimeter of blanket.
(For instructions on how to work embroidery stitches, see page 129.)

CUTTING TEMPLATE

25¾"

3½"

1"　　　　　　　　34"　　　　　　　　1"

i-cord wrap bracelet & rings

THIS IS A great project for using up leftover yarn FROM OTHER PROJECTS. IT'S A SIMPLE MATTER OF knitting I-cord, felting it, ironing it flat (IF DESIRED), AND THEN attaching a snap. I LIKE TO FLATTEN MY FELTED I-CORD WITH A CRAFT IRON (A TOOL MEANT FOR IRONING TINY CORNERS ON SEWING PROJECTS). IT reduces bulk, AND MAKES THE PIECES MORE comfortable to wear.

FINISHED MEASUREMENTS

BRACELET:
¼ (⅜)" wide x 25" long, before felting
³⁄₁₆ (¼)" wide x 21" long, after felting

RINGS:
¼ (⅜)" wide x 2¾" around, before felting
Approximately ring size 7, after felting

Results will depend on felting conditions and time spent felting.

YARN
100% wool yarn, worsted-weight, non-washable: 2 to 3 yards per ring, 7 to 9 yards per bracelet. Shown in Malabrigo Yarn Worsted (100% merino; 215 yards / 100 grams) #35 frank ochre and #37 lettuce, and Louet Riverstone Chunky (100% wool; 165 yards / 100 grams) #49 charcoal

NEEDLES
Two double-pointed needles (dpn) size US 11 (8 mm)

NOTIONS
Tapestry needle
Small lingerie bag with zipper
Clover Mini Iron (available at fabric stores)
Size 14 long-prong snaps, silver: 1 set per bracelet
The Snap Setter
OPTIONAL: assorted beads and 6" length of craft wire, for embellishing rings

GAUGE
Exact gauge is not crucial for this project.

BRACELET
CO 2 (3) sts, leaving 6" tail. Work I-Cord (see Special Techniques, page 129) for 25". BO all sts. Thread CO tail onto tapestry needle, and sew CO edge to I-Cord to create a loop 2" long. Weave in loose ends.

RINGS

CO 2 (3) sts. Work I-Cord for 2¾". BO all sts, leaving 6" tail. Thread BO tail onto tapestry needle, and sew BO edge to CO edge to create a ring. Weave in loose ends.

FELTING

Put ring(s) and 1 or 2 bracelets in a lingerie bag. Felt following instructions in Felting Basics, page 8.

Note #1

Don't put more than 2 bracelets in a lingerie bag. They tend to tangle together and create a knot, resulting in unevenly felted bracelets.

Once pieces are sufficiently felted, allow to air-dry.

FINISHING

Preheat Mini Iron. Press pieces flat with Mini Iron. Let cool.

Note #2

Pressing the pieces flat makes it easier to attach the snaps for the bracelets. It also makes the bracelets or rings lie flat on your wrist or finger.

BRACELET

Using The Snap Setter, attach male half of snap ¼" from base of loop, as shown in diagram. Attach female half of snap ¼" from end of I-Cord, on same side as male half of snap.

To wear: Lay loop end flat on top of your wrist with the top of the loop farthest away from you. Wrap rest of felted I-Cord around your wrist and slip end through loop. Wrap back in the opposite direction around the underside of your wrist to the top side of your wrist, and snap closed.

RING

Using beads and craft wire, embellish felted ring as shown or as desired.

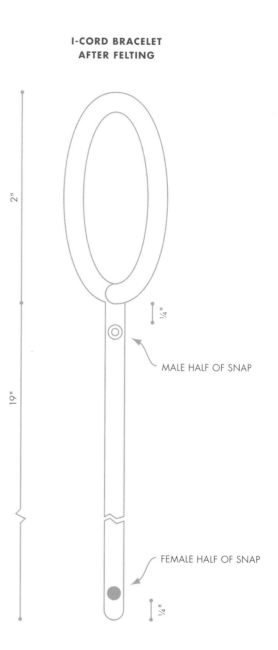

I-CORD WRAP BRACELET & RINGS

**I-CORD BRACELET
AFTER FELTING**

2"

19"

¼"

MALE HALF OF SNAP

FEMALE HALF OF SNAP

¼"

felted rings

— • —

THESE SIMPLE RINGS, *crafted from unspun wool, take less than 20 minutes to make,* PLUS DRYING TIME. *Leave them unadorned* OR *embellish with a contrasting color* OF WOOL AND EMBROIDERY THREAD, IF DESIRED.

....

FINISHED MEASUREMENTS
Sizes vary to fit finger

MATERIALS
Wool Mix by Leigh Radford (100% wool roving): one ½-ounce package makes approximately 12 rings. Samples shown in garni de fleurs.

NOTIONS
4 x 6 x 2" foam block. (Cut one end of block to measure 4 x ¾ x 2", then trim to 4 x ¾ x ¾".)
Two or three 36-gauge felting needles. (*While strong, these needles do tend to break, so it's a good idea to have extras on hand.*)
Liquid soap
32-ounce plastic bowl (Glad or Ziploc brand) with lid
Embroidery needle and floss

RING BASE
Follow instructions for Creating Needle-Felted Fabric in Felting Basics, page 15, to create piece of needle-felted wool measuring 2½" long, ¼" wide at ends, and up to ½" wide at center if embellishment will be added (see diagram for ring shape templates). Place partially felted wool around finger to check for size. Overlap ends so ring fits around finger loosely (as you continue needle-felting process, ring will continue to shrink). Needle felt section of ring where ends overlap, slipping ring onto finger frequently to check for size. Once ring is correct size, set aside to dry or embellish further.

Note #1
Slipping your small foam block through the center of your ring base (or slipping the ring base over a corner of the block) will help you needle felt around the entire perimeter of your ring.

EMBELLISHING WITH MULTIPLE BOBBLES
Roll a very small amount of dampened contrast-color roving between your fingers to create a small ball, about the size of a pea or slightly smaller. Continue rolling until ball reaches desired size and smoothness. Repeat, creating 5 bobbles (or desired number of bobbles). Set ring base and bobbles aside to dry.

Note #2
Make sure all your pieces are dry prior to assembly.

Thread embroidery needle with contrasting color of floss. Insert needle from WS of ring base through to RS. Insert needle through first bobble. Reinsert needle through bobble and ring base, from RS to WS, ⅛" away from previous insertion point. Repeat for desired number of bobbles.

Note #3

Depending on thickness of stitching desired, you can use a full strand of embroidery floss, or you can separate the floss and use a smaller number of plies.

EMBELLISHING WITH A SINGLE BOBBLE

Following instructions above, roll a single bobble, adding roving if needed to create desired size. Attach to ring base with either a basic setting or a channel setting.

BASIC SETTING: Place bobble on top of ring base, in center or in desired position. Thread embroidery needle with contrasting color of floss. *Insert needle from WS of ring base up through ring base and bobble. Reinsert needle through bobble and ring base, from RS to WS, ¼" away from prior insertion point. Repeat from *, positioning needle in same 2 insertion points each time, until floss is desired thickness.

CHANNEL SETTING: With 2" length of dampened roving the same color as ring base, roll lengthwise so that roving begins to resemble the shape of a toothpick. Insert small foam block through the center of your ring base (or slip ring base over a corner of the block). Bend toothpick-shaped section of roving into a circle and place on top of your ring base (see diagram), to form a channel setting to hold felted bobble. With felting needle, poke the base of the channel setting to attach it to your ring base. Place bobble into the channel setting and needle felt until bobble is secured to the ring base.

Note #4

Needle felting the bobble into place can be difficult. To ensure bobble is secure, tack into place: insert threaded embroidery needle from WS of ring base up into bottom portion of bobble, and back to WS of ring base.

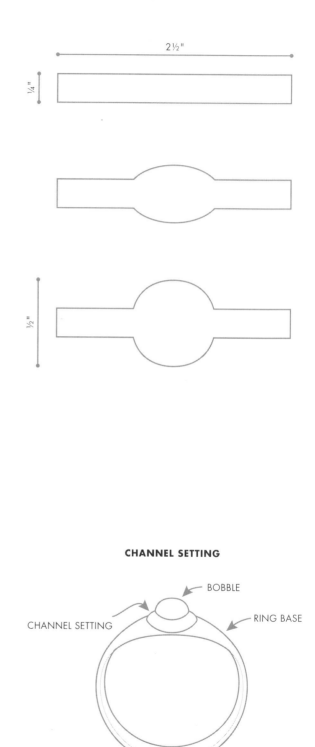

RING SHAPE TEMPLATES

CHANNEL SETTING

necklace

—•—

SOMETIMES *the projects that are the most fun* TO MAKE RELY ON THE MOST *basic techniques.* HERE, I'VE CREATED A SIMPLE *felt rectangle,* EMBELLISHED IT WITH *beads,* AND HUNG IT ON LEATHER LACING.

....

FINISHED MEASUREMENTS

1½ x 3¾"

Results will depend on felting conditions and time spent felting.

MATERIALS

Wool Mix by Leigh Radford (100% wool roving): one ½-ounce package makes 3 necklaces. Shown in garnet.

NOTIONS

Two or three 36-gauge felting needles. *(While strong, these needles do tend to break, so it's a good idea to have extras on hand.)*

4 x 6 x 2" foam block

Liquid soap

32-ounce plastic bowl (Glad or Ziploc brand) with lid

Sewing needle

Top-stitching thread or embroidery floss to match roving

16 silver beads: eight ⅛" solid circles, one ¼" solid circle, six ½" open circles, and one ⅜" solid square (available at bead stores; see Sources for Supplies, page 132)

5 split jump rings, silver

Flat-nose pliers

1¾ x 4" piece of silk fabric

Fabric scissors and straight pins

36" round leather cord

Multipurpose cement

Hook-and-eye clasp with crimp ends

NECKLACE BASE

Follow instructions for Creating Needle-Felted Fabric in Felting Basics, page 15, to create piece of needle-felted wool measuring 1½ x 3¾". Once piece is desired shape and thickness, set aside to air-dry.

FINISHING

Insert threaded sewing needle from WS of necklace base through to RS, and sew beads as shown or in desired pattern.

Note

I chose to wrap my sewing thread around the topside of some of my beads for a decorative effect.

Create a very small opening in each jump ring by gently bending ring away from you at the split with flat-nose pliers. Slip open end of first jump ring through top edge of necklace base at center point. With pliers, completely close jump ring. Repeat with 2 more jump rings positioned on each side of center jump ring. With threaded sewing needle, reinforce each jump ring by inserting needle through WS of necklace base and jump ring 2 or 3 times.

NECKLACE BACKING: Cut piece of silk fabric to measure ¼" larger in width and length than necklace base. With warm iron, and WS of fabric facing you, fold edges over ¼" and press. Place WS of silk on top of WS of necklace and secure with straight pins. With threaded sewing needle, sew silk backing to necklace base.

ASSEMBLY: Cut leather cord to 36". Slip cord through jump rings, placing necklace in the center. Dab small amount of cement on first end of cord, then slip end into hole at clasp base. Holding end firmly in place, firmly crimp clamp base with pliers. Attach second half of clasp to opposite end of cord as for first end. Dry overnight.

basic needle-felted pullovers

— • —

I CHOSE TO WORK THESE PULLOVERS IN THE ROUND (*no seams to sew!*) AND IN A SOLID COLOR AND THEN *add my motif using needle felting* ONCE THE KNITTING WAS COMPLETED. NEEDLE FELTING IS A GREAT WAY TO ADD A GRAPHIC ELEMENT TO YOUR KNITTING WITHOUT HAVING TO MANAGE MULTIPLE STRANDS OF YARN. YOU CAN CHOOSE TO WORK A MOTIF THAT *covers the entire yoke of this sweater,* *or work a series of smaller designs* ON THE FRONT YOKE, SLEEVE, OR CENTER BACK.

FINISHED MEASUREMENTS
26 (28, 30, 32, 34, 36, 38, 40, 42, 44, 46)" chest

YARN
Rowan Scottish Tweed Aran (100% wool; 186 yards / 100 grams): 2 (3, 3, 4, 4, 5, 5, 6, 6, 6, 7) skeins. Size 26" shown in #013 claret. Size 30" shown in #032 Lewis blue. Size 46" shown in #009 rust.

NEEDLES
One 24" or 29" circular needle size US 8 (5 mm)
One 24" or 29" circular needle size US 9 (5.5 mm)
One set of 4 or 5 double-pointed needles (dpn) size US 8 (5 mm)
One set of 4 or 5 double-pointed needles (dpn) size US 9 (5.5 mm)
Change needle size if necessary to obtain the correct gauge.

NOTIONS
Stitch markers
Stitch holders or waste yarn
Tapestry needle
Wool Mix by Leigh Radford (100% wool roving): one 2-ounce package. Sizes 26" and 30" shown in Bainbridge Island. Size 46" shown in Eagle Creek.
Two to three 36-gauge felting needles. (*While strong, these needles do tend to break, so it's a good idea to have extras on hand.*)

GAUGE
16 sts and 24 rows = 4" (10 cm) in Stockinette stitch (St st) using larger needles

BODY
Using smaller circular needle, CO 104 (112, 120, 128, 136, 144, 152, 160, 168, 176, 184) sts. Join for working in the rnd, being careful not to twist sts; place marker (pm) for beginning of rnd at left side "seam."

HEM: Work 4 (4, 4, 4, 4, 6, 6, 6, 6, 6, 6) rnds of St st. Purl 1 rnd. Change to larger circular needle and work 4 (4, 4, 4, 4, 6, 6, 6, 6, 6, 6) rnds of St st. Next Rnd: *With left-hand needle, pick up 1 st from CO edge, knit picked-up st together with next st on left-hand needle; repeat from * around.

Work in St st, placing additional marker at right side "seam" after 52 (56, 60, 64, 68, 72, 76, 80, 84, 88, 92) sts. Work even until body measures 8½ (9½, 11, 12¾, 14, 14, 14, 14½, 15, 15¾, 16)", ending 3 (3, 4, 4, 4, 4, 4, 5, 5, 6, 6) sts before marker at left side "seam."

DIVIDE FOR FRONT AND BACK: BO 6 (6, 8, 8, 8, 8, 8, 10, 10, 12, 12) sts, knit to 3 (3, 4, 4, 4, 4, 4, 5, 5, 6, 6) sts before next marker, BO 6 (6, 8, 8, 8, 8, 8, 10, 10, 12, 12) sts, knit across back—46 (50, 52, 56, 60, 64, 68, 70, 74, 76, 80) sts in front and in back. Transfer sts to st holder or waste yarn, and set aside.

SLEEVES (make 2)

Using smaller dpns, CO 24 (26, 28, 30, 32, 38, 38, 40, 40, 42, 44) sts. Divide sts evenly among 3 or 4 dpns. Join for working in the rnd, being careful not to twist sts; pm for beginning of rnd.

HEM: Work 4 (4, 4, 4, 4, 6, 6, 6, 6, 6, 6) rnds of St st. Purl 1 rnd. Change to larger dpns and work 4 (4, 4, 4, 4, 6, 6, 6, 6, 6, 6) rnds of St st.

Next Rnd: *With left-hand needle, pick up 1 st from CO edge, knit picked-up st together with next st on left-hand needle; repeat from * around.

SLEEVE SHAPING: Work even in St st for 1½ (1½, 1½, 2, 2, 2, 2½, 2½, 2½, 2½, 2½)". Increase 1 st each side of marker every 6 (6, 6, 6, 7, 9, 8, 7, 7, 7, 8) rnds 7 (8, 9, 9, 10, 8, 9, 10, 11, 11, 11) times— 38 (42, 46, 48, 52, 54, 56, 60, 62, 64, 66) sts.

Work even until sleeve measures 11½ (12¼, 13, 14½, 15¾, 17, 17½, 18, 18½, 19, 20)" from purl rnd of hem, ending 3 (3, 4, 4, 4, 4, 4, 5, 5, 6, 6) sts before marker. BO 6 (6, 8, 8, 8, 8, 8, 10, 10, 12, 12) sts, knit to end—32 (36, 38, 40, 44, 46, 48, 50, 52, 52, 54) sts.

YOKE

With RS facing, join pieces as follows: Knit across sts of left sleeve, pm, knit across sts of front, pm, knit across sts of right sleeve, pm, knit across sts of back, pm—156 (172, 180, 192, 208, 220, 232, 240, 252, 256, 268) sts. Attach removable marker or piece of waste yarn to this rnd to indicate base of yoke.

Next Rnd: Decrease 1 (2, 0, 2, 3, 0, 2, 0, 2, 1, 3) sts as evenly as possible, placing decreases near sleeve/body joins so they will be less noticeable—155 (170, 180, 190, 205, 220, 230, 240, 250, 255, 265) sts.

Work even until yoke measures 1½ (1¾, 2, 2, 2, 2, 2, 2, 2½, 2½, 2½)". Decrease Rnd 1: *K3, k2tog; repeat from * around—124 (136, 144, 152, 164, 176, 184, 192, 200, 204, 212) sts.

Work even until yoke measures 2¾ (3¼, 3¾, 4, 4, 4, 4½, 4½, 4¾, 5, 5)". Decrease Rnd 2: *K2, k2tog; repeat from * around—93 (102, 108, 114, 123, 132, 138, 144, 150, 153, 159) sts.

Work even until yoke measures 4 (4¾, 5¼, 5¾, 6, 6, 6½, 6½, 7, 7, 7)". Decrease Rnd 3: *K1, k2tog; repeat from * around—62 (68, 72, 76, 82, 88, 92, 96, 100, 102, 106) sts.

Work even until yoke measures 5 (5¾, 6¼, 7, 7¾, 8, 8½, 9, 9¼, 9½, 9½)".

NECK SHAPING: Raise back neck with short rows (see Special Techniques, page 129) as follows:

Row 1 (RS): Knit to 2 sts before back left shoulder marker, wrp-t.
Row 2 (WS): Purl to 2 sts before back right shoulder marker, wrp-t.
Row 3: Knit to 4 sts before previous wrapped st, wrp-t.
Row 4: Purl to 4 sts before previous wrapped st, wrp-t.
FOR SIZE 38" AND LARGER ONLY: Repeat Rows 3 and 4.

Knit 1 rnd, working each wrap together with the st it wraps (see Special Techniques, page 129).

NECKBAND: Change to smaller needles. Work k1, p1 rib for ½ (½, ¾, ¾, ¾, 1, 1, 1, 1, 1, 1)" or desired length. BO all sts loosely in pattern.

FINISHING

With tapestry needle threaded with yarn, sew underarm seams. Weave in loose ends. Block to measurements.

NEEDLE FELTING

Following Needle-Felting directions in Felting Basics on page 14, work needle-felt designs as shown in diagrams. Work from center of each motif towards its outer edge, being careful not to stretch the surface of your knit fabric.

Each motif has been designed to fit sweaters in a variety of sizes. In addition, you can adjust the motif placed across the yoke by adding or removing geometric shapes at the outer edges of the motif.

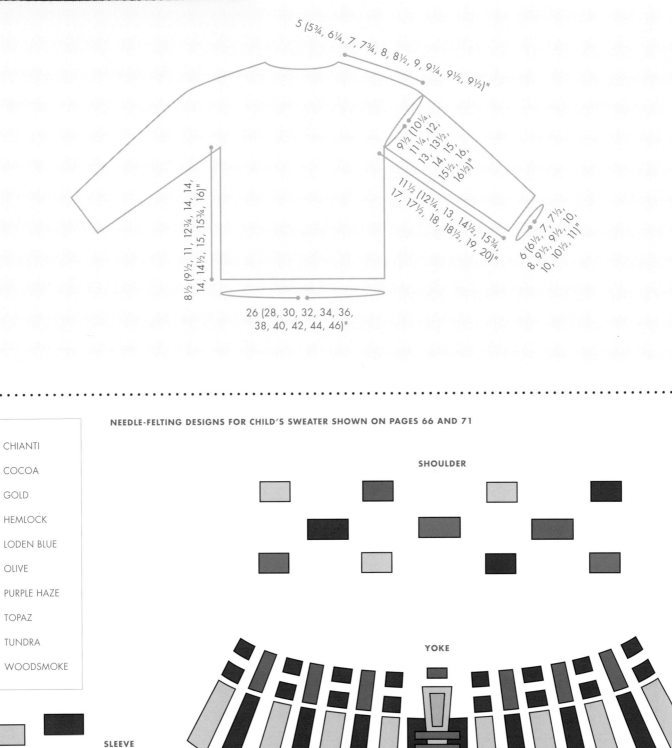

5 (5¾, 6¼, 7, 7¾, 8, 8½, 9, 9¼, 9½, 9½)"

9½ (10¼, 12, 11¼, 13½, 13, 15, 14, 16, 15½, 16½)"

8½ (9½, 11, 12¾, 14, 14, 14, 14½, 15, 15¾, 16)"

11½ (12¼, 13, 14½, 15¾, 17, 17½, 18, 18½, 19, 20)"

6 (6½, 7, 7½, 8, 9½, 9½, 10, 10, 10½, 11)"

26 (28, 30, 32, 34, 36, 38, 40, 42, 44, 46)"

NEEDLE-FELTING DESIGNS FOR CHILD'S SWEATER SHOWN ON PAGES 66 AND 71

CHIANTI

COCOA

GOLD

HEMLOCK

LODEN BLUE

OLIVE

PURPLE HAZE

TOPAZ

TUNDRA

WOODSMOKE

SHOULDER

YOKE

SLEEVE

NEEDLE-FELTING DESIGNS FOR ADULT
SWEATER SHOWN ON PAGE 66

YOKE

SLEEVE

NEEDLE-FELTING DESIGNS FOR CHILD'S SWEATER SHOWN ON PAGE 69

YOKE

CENTER BACK

SLEEVE

needle-felted pillows

I GET A LOT OF PLEASURE OUT OF *knitting with color,* BUT I DON'T ALWAYS WANT TO FOLLOW A CHART OR THINK TOO HARD ABOUT WHAT I'M DOING. *For laid-back times like that, these pillows are perfect.* FIRST I *knit two pillow covers in solid colors;* LATER ON I *add a more intricate design* WITH ROVING AND A FELTING NEEDLE.

FINISHED MEASUREMENTS
14 x 14", after assembling

YARN
Harrisville Designs New England Highland (100% wool; 200 yards / 100 grams): 1 hank each of 3 colors for each pillow. Pillow One shown in #19 blackberry (A), #20 purple haze (B), and #7 tundra (C). Pillow Two shown in #20 purple haze (A), #26 wedgewood (B), and #7 tundra (C).

Note #1

One hank of #7 tundra will complete both pillows as shown.

NEEDLES
One pair straight needles size US 10 (6 mm)
One pair straight needles size US 9 (5.5 mm)
Change needle size if necessary to obtain the correct gauge.

NOTIONS
Tapestry needle
Sewing needle, thread, and pins
Eight 1" buttons (4 for each pillow)
Wool Mix by Leigh Radford (100% wool roving): one 2-ounce package for each pillow. Pillow One shown in Willamette Valley. Pillow Two shown in Irvington.
Two or three 36-gauge felting needles. *(While strong, these needles do tend to break, so it's a good idea to have extras on hand.)*

9 x 12 x 2" foam felting block
Two 14 x 14" pillow forms

GAUGE
15 ½ sts and 22 rows = 4" (10 cm) in Stockinette stitch (St st) using larger needles

PILLOW
LOWER BACK: Using smaller needles and A, CO 56 sts. Work 4 rows Garter st. Change to St st and work even until piece measures 1" from CO edge. Change to larger needles, and continuing in St st, work even until piece measures 10¾" from CO edge, ending with a WS row.

FRONT: Change to B and work even for 14"; end with a WS row.

UPPER BACK: Change to C and work even for 4", ending with a WS row. Change to smaller needles and work buttonholes as follows:
Row 1 (RS): K8, *BO 4, K8 (including 1 st on right-hand needle); repeat from * to end.
Row 2: *P8, CO 4; repeat from * to last 8 sts, p8.

Work 2 more rows of St st. Change to B and work 2 rows Garter st. BO all sts.

FINISHING

ASSEMBLY: Block to measurements. Fold pillow at color changes, overlapping Upper Back over Lower Back by 1¾", and pin in place. With tapestry needle threaded with yarn, using mattress st (see Special Techniques, page 129), sew side seams. Weave in loose ends. With sewing needle and thread, sew buttons in place.

NEEDLE FELTING: Work needle-felting designs as shown in diagrams, following instructions in Felting Basics on page 14.

Note # 2

Needle felting after assembling the pillow will give you a better perspective of the overall design, allowing you to place design elements exactly where they will appear in the finished pillow. If you would rather, of course, you may needle felt prior to assembling the pillow.

Insert pillow form.

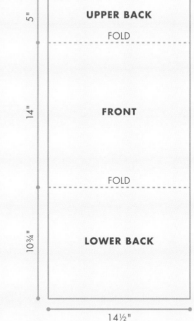

5" — UPPER BACK

FOLD

14" — FRONT

FOLD

10¾" — LOWER BACK

14½"

ASTER

BLACKBERRY

DOVE GREY

GARNET

HEMLOCK

PURPLE HAZE

TUNDRA

WEDGEWOOD

WHITE

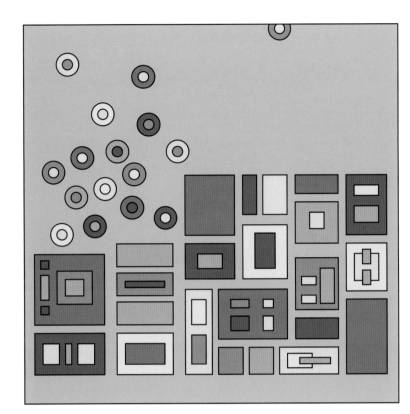

willamette wrap

— • —

INSPIRED BY A PARTICULARLY BEAUTIFUL CLOUDY DAY HERE IN THE *Willamette Valley in Oregon,* I CHOSE A *creamy color of an alpaca-silk blend yarn* FOR THIS GARTER-STITCH CARDIGAN THAT DRAPES AT AN ANGLE WHEN WORN. THE COLLAR IS *needle felted in layers with merino-silk roving* AND THEN CLOSED WITH A LARGE PIN.

....

FINISHED MEASUREMENTS
33 (37½, 42)" chest

YARN
Blue Sky Alpacas Alpaca Silk (50% alpaca, 50% silk; 146 yards / 50 grams): 11 (13, 16) hanks #110 ecru

NEEDLES
One 24" or 29" circular needle size US 6 (4 mm)
Change needle size if necessary to obtain the correct gauge.

NOTIONS
Stitch holders or waste yarn
Tapestry needle
Blocking wires (see Sources for Supplies, page 132)
Louet Merino/Silk Top (80% merino, 20% silk): ½ ounce natural
Clover felting tool
Two or three 36-gauge felting needles. *(While strong, these needles do tend to break, so it's a good idea to have extras on hand.)*
9 x 12 x 2" foam felting block
Decorative pin for closure

GAUGE
21 sts and 45 rows = 4" (10 cm) in Garter stitch

BODY
CO 173 (197, 221) sts. Work in Garter st, keeping first st and last st in St st (knit on RS, purl on WS), until body measures 10 (11½, 13)", ending with a WS row.

Next RS row, divide back and fronts as follows: Work 40 (46, 50) sts of right front in pattern, then transfer to st holder or waste yarn. BO 8 (10, 12) sts at right armhole, work to last 48 (56, 62) sts, then transfer 77 (85, 97) sts of back to st holder or waste yarn. BO 8 (10, 12) sts at left armhole, and work to end of row.

LEFT FRONT
Continuing in Garter st and keeping first st and last st in St st, decrease 1 st at armhole edge on next 2 (2, 4) RS rows—38 (44, 46) sts. Work even until armhole measures 6¾ (7¾, 8)", ending with a WS row. Transfer sts to st holder or waste yarn.

BACK
Join yarn at left armhole. Continuing in Garter st and keeping first st and last st in St st, decrease 1 st at each armhole edge on next 2 (2, 4) RS rows—73 (81, 89) sts. Work even until armhole measures 6¾ (7¾, 8)", ending with a WS row. Transfer sts to st holder or waste yarn.

RIGHT FRONT
Join yarn at right armhole. Continuing in Garter st and keeping first st and last st in St st, decrease 1 st at armhole edge on next 2 (2, 4) RS rows—38 (44, 46) sts. Work even until armhole measures 6¾ (7¾, 8)", ending with a WS row.

COLLAR

Continuing in Garter st and keeping first st and last st in St st, work across sts of right front, CO 8 (10, 12) sts, work across sts of back, CO 8 (10, 12) sts, work across sts of left front—165 (189, 205) sts. Work even for 1", ending with a RS row. Keeping first st and last st in St st, work remaining sts as follows:

Row 1 (WS): Knit.
Row 2 (RS): Knit.
Row 3: Purl.
Rows 4-6: Knit.
Rows 7-9: Purl.
Row 10: Knit.

Work in St st for 3¾", ending with a RS row. Keeping first st and last st in St st, work remaining sts as follows:

Row 1 (WS): Knit.
Row 2: Knit.
Row 3: Purl.
Rows 4-5: Knit.

BO all sts knitwise.

SLEEVES (make 2)

CO 43 (45, 47) sts. Work in Garter st, keeping first st and last st in St st (knit on RS, purl on WS), until sleeve measures 2½"; end ready to work a RS row. Increase 1 st at each edge every 16 (14, 12) rows 10 (12, 15) times—63 (69, 77) sts. Work even until sleeve measures 17 (18, 19)", ending with a RS row.

SHAPE CAP: BO 4 (5, 6) sts at beginning of next 2 rows—55 (59, 65) sts. Decrease 1 st at each edge every row 4 times, then every 5 rows 11 (13, 14) times—25 (25, 29) sts. BO 3 sts at beginning of next 2 rows, then BO remaining 19 (19, 23) sts.

FINISHING

Weave in loose ends. Block all pieces using blocking wires. With tapestry needle threaded with yarn, sew in sleeves.

NEEDLE FELTING COLLAR

Following instructions for needle felting on knit fabric in Felting Basics section on page 14, cover St st section of collar (as indicated on schematic) with merino/silk roving. Alternate use of Clover felting tool and individual felting needle until entire St st section is covered.

Note

The roving is going to react to being dampened and poked with the felting needles by not laying perfectly flat while you are working. I chose to let the fiber create its own natural pattern as I covered the collar area.

Once collar is sufficiently felted, lay flat to dry, using blocking wires if necessary to block the collar area evenly.

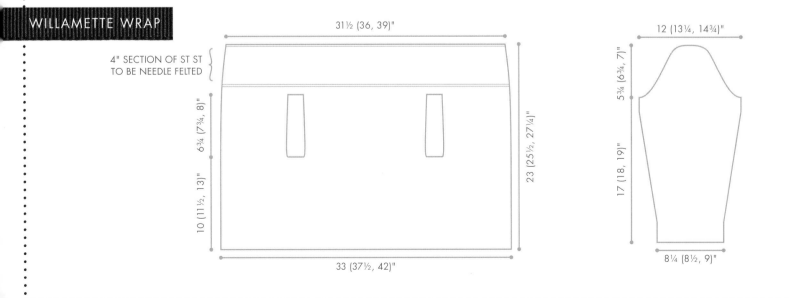

WILLAMETTE WRAP

market bag

My first forays into needle felting were on knitted fabric, AND I WAS DELIGHTED WHEN I REALIZED THAT I COULD ALSO NEEDLE FELT ON WOVEN FABRIC. FOR THIS STURDY BAG, I CHOSE midweight upholstery fabric. USING ITS floral pattern AS MY GUIDE, I filled in with wool roving and embroidery floss.

FINISHED MEASUREMENTS

15" wide, when laid flat
15" tall, from base to top of bag

MATERIALS

¾ yard upholstery fabric

NOTIONS

Fabric scissors
Dressmaker's pencil
Sewing machine, thread, and pins
Iron
Wool Mix by Leigh Radford (100% wool roving): one 1-ounce package. Shown in woodland colorway.
Two or three 32- or 36-gauge felting needles. *(While strong, these needles do tend to break, so it's a good idea to have extras on hand.)*
4 x 6 x 2" foam felting block
DMC embroidery floss (shown in colors #169, #834, and #3799; 1 skein each)
Embroidery needle

FABRIC PREPARATION

Cut fabric for body of bag, facing, and handles as shown in Step 1.

Note

Upholstery fabric has a tendency to unravel. Machine-zigzag around the edges of your fabric to keep the edges from unraveling.

BAG

Fold rectangle in half with RS's together and pin on right and left edges. With dressmaker's pencil, draw a horizontal line at fold line marking the bottom of bag. Machine-sew side seams with ½" seam allowance. Press seams open. Flatten bottom of bag so that side seams line up with horizontal line marking bottom of bag, creating triangular flap at each end of bottom of bag. Machine-sew a short seam across each triangular flap approximately 2½" from endpoint, to form bottom and side gussets for bag, as shown in Step 2. Turn bag RS out.

HANDLES *(make 2)*

Fold long edges of handle under ¼" and press with warm iron. Fold handle in half lengthwise and pin into place. Machine-topstitch folded edges together—finished handle measures 1⅛ x 24". On RS, pin handle to top edge of bag as shown in Step 3. Repeat for second handle.

FACING

Place facing pieces with RS's together. Machine-sew seams along short edges, with ½" seam allowance. Press seams open. With RS's together, slip facing over top of bag, matching side seams of facing and bag. Pin facing into place. Machine-stitch facing into place with ½" seam allowance, securing handles to bag, as shown in Step 4.

Fold unfinished edge of facing under ¼" and press. Turn facing to inside of bag. With RS of bag facing you, topstitch through body of bag and facing twice: once ⅛" in from folded edge of facing, and again ⅛" in from top edge of bag.

EMBELLISHMENT

Needle felt design on upholstery fabric as desired using wool roving and felting needle, following instructions in Felting Basics on page 14.

Embroider French knots as desired (see Special Techniques, page 129), using full strand of embroidery floss threaded onto embroidery needle.

MARKET BAG

STEP 1

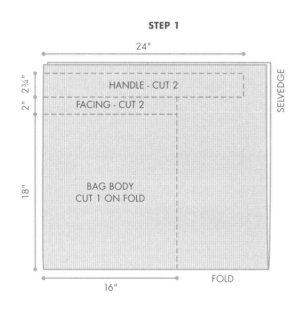

24"

2" 2¾"

HANDLE - CUT 2

FACING - CUT 2

18"

BAG BODY
CUT 1 ON FOLD

SELVEDGE

16"

FOLD

STEP 2

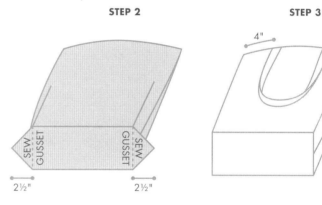

SEW GUSSET

SEW GUSSET

2½"

2½"

STEP 3

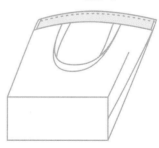

4"

4"

STEP 4

- - - CUT

· · · · SEW

☐ RIGHT SIDE OF FABRIC

▦ WRONG SIDE OF FABRIC

blue jay blanket

•—•

I COMPLETED MANY OF THE PROJECTS IN THIS BOOK SITTING ON MY BACK PORCH, OFTEN ACCOMPANIED BY A VERY LARGE *blue jay who would boss around the other birds* FROM *his perch on the maple tree,* SO IT'S NOT SURPRISING THAT WHEN IT CAME TIME TO CHOOSE A *motif to needle felt onto this throw,* THE IDEA OF A BLUE JAY CAME TO MIND. I LOVE THE JUXTAPOSITION OF THE *serious wool suiting fabric with the folkloric needle-felted blue jay* AND SIMPLE EMBROIDERED EMBELLISHMENTS.

....

FINISHED MEASUREMENTS
57 x 71"

MATERIALS
2 yards wool (suit weight) fabric, 58" or 60" wide
2 yards backing fabric, 58" or 60" wide

NOTIONS
Fabric scissors
Wool Mix by Leigh Radford (100% wool roving): one 1-ounce package; sample shown in blue jay
Two or three 36-gauge felting needles. *(While strong, these needles do tend to break, so it's a good idea to have extras on hand.)*
9 x 12 x 2" foam felting block
DMC embroidery floss (shown in colors #581 green, #30762 white, and #30414 blue; 1 skein each)
Embroidery needle
Sewing machine and thread
Iron
Hand-sewing needle

Note #1
I've chosen to use a suit-weight wool fabric for my throw. While wool fabric is best, most woven fabric will work. The best way to ensure the fabric you are considering will work is to needle felt a test piece.

Note #2
For the backing fabric, select a lightweight or midweight fabric that, when combined with your top fabric, won't make your finished throw too heavy.

FABRIC PREPARATION
Cut wool suiting fabric and backing fabric to measure 58" wide x 72" long.

NEEDLE FELTING AND EMBROIDERY
Needle felt flower and bird designs on wool suiting fabric according to diagrams, following instructions in Felting Basics on page 14.

Using full strand of embroidery floss threaded onto embroidery needle, embroider flower and bird designs on wool suiting fabric, and dragonfly design onto backing fabric, according to diagrams.

ASSEMBLY
With RS's together, machine-sew wool suiting fabric and backing fabric together, using a ½" seam allowance and leaving a 12" opening. Turn throw RS-out through opening, and press with warm iron. Hand-sew opening closed.

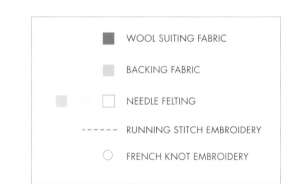

■	WOOL SUITING FABRIC
■	BACKING FABRIC
■ □	NEEDLE FELTING
-----	RUNNING STITCH EMBROIDERY
○	FRENCH KNOT EMBROIDERY

EMBROIDERY DESIGN

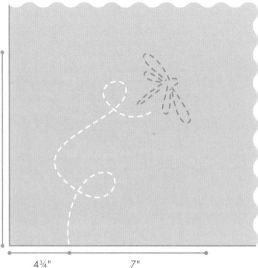

25"

4¾"   7"

15"

4"

16"

NEEDLE-FELTING DESIGNS

25"

4¾"   21¾"

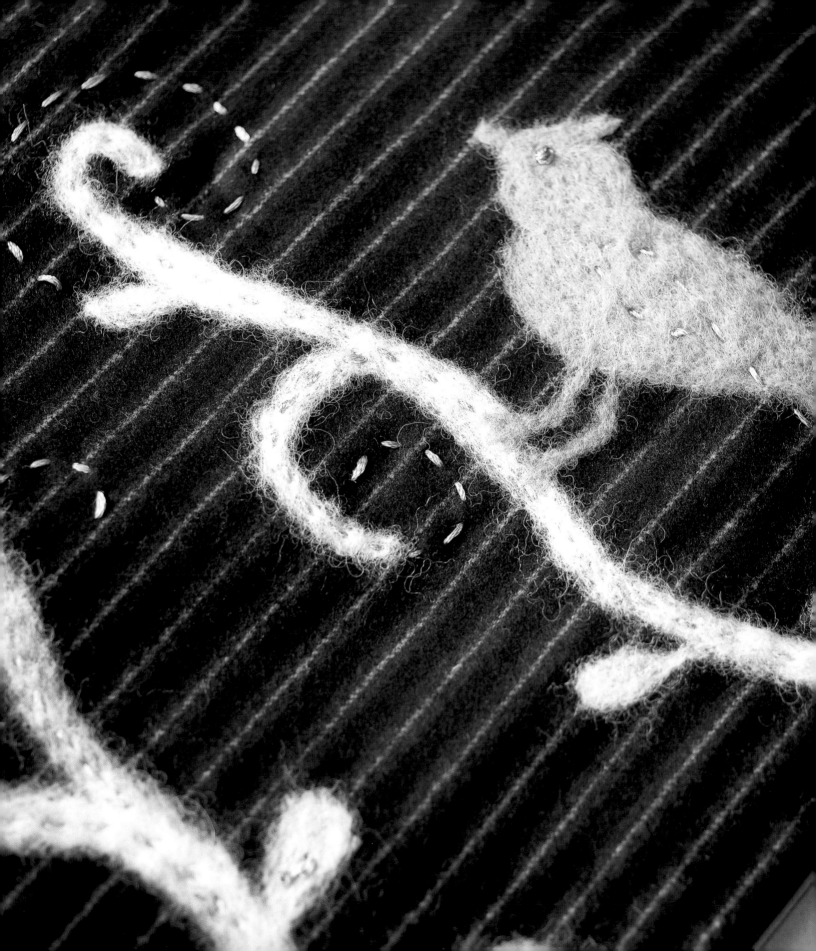

pincushions

BRIGHTLY *embellished with contrasting roving,* THESE PINCUSHIONS ARE AN *artful way to store straight pins.* I LIKE TO KEEP A COUPLE ON HAND FOR *last-minute gifts for my crafty friends.*

FINISHED MEASUREMENTS
3½" diameter (results will depend on felting conditions and time spent felting)

MATERIALS
Wool Mix Pincushion Kit (100% wool roving): one 2-ounce package makes 3 pincushions

NOTIONS
Liquid soap
32-ounce plastic bowl (Glad or Ziploc brand) with lid
Rubber gloves with textured palms (for friction and faster felting)
Two to three 36-gauge felting needles

SOLID-COLOR PINCUSHION
Fill bowl with very hot, soapy water. A few drops of soap is sufficient; the water shouldn't be slippery to the touch.

Put on dishwashing gloves and dampen palms with hot water from bowl. Fluff a handful of roving by pulling into sections. Gather roving into a soft ball. Very gently, roll ball between palms. Dip ball into hot water just to dampen surface, and continue to roll. Add additional pieces of roving crosswise if you want to increase ball size. As ball solidifies you can increase amount of pressure used.

Note

If your pincushion begins to form a crack, add a piece of torn roving lengthwise over the crack and another crosswise, and resume rolling. Repeat until crack is sufficiently covered.

Keep water hot by placing lid on bowl as you work, and adding more hot water as necessary. If water cools, roving will felt more slowly. You can also add a few drops of soap directly to your roving. If pincushion gets too sudsy, rinse it under faucet or swish around in water bowl.

Continue to roll pincushion between palms until it reaches desired smoothness and size. Rinse with cold water and gently squeeze out excess water. Press down on cushion with hand to flatten. Set aside to air-dry.

MULTICOLOR PINCUSHION
For pincushion with design in contrasting color, follow directions for solid-color pincushion until partially felted— still quite soft to touch, but with shape fully formed. Choose a contrasting roving color, dampen in soapy water, and place in desired position. Using felting needle, gently poke roving until design is securely in place. Continue to roll pincushion between palms until it is desired smoothness and size.

For pincushion that has appearance of a two-color base, follow directions for solid-color pincushion until desired size. Cover half of pincushion with contrasting roving color and continue to roll between palms, adding additional roving as necessary for desired coverage.

balls & buttons

—·—

I LOVE MAKING THESE DECORATIVE BALLS AND BUTTONS AND *experimenting with different color combinations and surface designs.* SET THE BALLS ON A TABLE SO YOU CAN PLAY WITH OR ADMIRE THEM WHENEVER YOU LIKE, *string them together to create decorative garland* (SEE PAGE 94), OR HANG THEM AS *ornaments* (AS SHOWN ON PAGE 96). INSTRUCTIONS FOR ALL OF THESE OPTIONS ARE INCLUDED IN THE PATTERN. THE BUTTONS ARE MADE PRETTY MUCH THE SAME WAY AS THE BALLS EXCEPT, PARTWAY THROUGH THE FELTING PROCESS, THE *balls are placed in the freezer for 10 minutes and cut in half,* THEN WHEN DRY, *jump rings are attached to the backs* TO ACT AS SHAFTS SO *they can be sewn onto clothing or anything else.* PERSONALLY, I LIKE HOW *unexpected and unique they look on nonknitted garments* LIKE THE JACKET IN THE PHOTO ON PAGE 92.

....

FINISHED MEASUREMENTS
Balls: ½ to 1" diameter
Buttons: 1 to 1½" diameter
Results will depend on felting conditions and time
spent felting.

MATERIALS
Wool Mix by Leigh Radford (100% wool roving): one 2-ounce
package makes approximately twenty-eight 1" balls or twenty-
eight ½" buttons.

NOTIONS
Liquid soap
32-ounce plastic bowl (Glad or Ziploc brand) with lid
Rubber gloves with textured palms (for friction and faster felting)
Two or three 36-gauge felting needles. *(While strong, these
needles do tend to break, so it's a good idea to have extras on
hand.)*

FOR ORNAMENTS OR GARLAND ONLY:
Linen or hemp yarn: 10" for each ornament or approximately
18' for garland
Tapestry needle

FOR BUTTONS ONLY:
Access to kitchen freezer
Cutting board
Sharp, non-serrated knife
Sewing needle
Embroidery floss
Jump rings

SOLID-COLOR BALLS
Fill bowl with very hot, soapy water. A few drops of soap is
sufficient; the water shouldn't be slippery to the touch.

Wearing a pair of dishwashing gloves, dampen the palms of your gloves with hot water from bowl. Fluff a small amount of roving (about the size of an egg) by pulling into sections. Gather roving into a soft ball. Very gently, roll ball between your palms, being careful not to exert too much pressure (the key to a smooth surface is to use a very light touch at the beginning of the process). Dip ball into hot water just to dampen the surface, and continue to roll. Add additional pieces of fluffed-up roving in a crosswise fashion if you would like to increase the size of your ball. As the ball begins to take shape and become more solid, you can increase the amount of pressure used.

Note

If your ball begins to form a crack, add a piece of torn roving lengthwise over the crack and another crosswise, and resume rolling. Repeat until crack is sufficiently covered.

Keep water hot by placing lid on bowl as you work, and adding more hot water as necessary. If the water begins to cool, the rate at which your work felts will slow down.

You can also add a few drops of soap directly to your roving. If you add too much soap and get lots of suds, rinse the ball under a faucet or swish it around in your bowl of water.

Continue to roll ball between your palms until it reaches desired smoothness and size. Rinse felted ball with cold water, and *gently* squeeze out excess water. Set aside to air-dry.

MULTICOLOR BALLS

Follow directions for solid-color balls until partially felted—still quite soft to the touch, but with the shape of the ball fully formed. Choose a contrasting color, dampen in soapy water, and place in desired position on felted ball. Using felting needle, gently poke roving until design is securely in place. Continue to roll ball between the palms of your hands until ball is desired smoothness and size.

FINISHING BALLS

ORNAMENTS: Thread 10" of yarn onto tapestry needle. Insert needle up through one or more felted balls, then back down in the opposite direction, leaving a 2½" loop at the top. Tie knot in yarn at base of ornament to secure.

GARLAND: Using tapestry needle, string felted balls onto yarn, spacing them approximately 2½ to 3" apart. Tie a knot on each side of each ball to secure in place.

SOLID-COLOR BUTTONS

Follow directions for solid-color balls until balls are approximately ¾ felted. Place balls into freezer for 10 to 15 minutes. Remove from freezer and place balls on cutting board, and cut each ball in half with knife. Return cut balls to hot, soapy water and continue to roll gently to smooth out the cut edges and create a more finished surface. When buttons are desired smoothness, rinse with cold water. Gently flatten and refine shape as necessary. Set aside to air-dry.

MARBLED BUTTONS

Follow directions for solid-color buttons, but add small amounts of constrasting colors as you work, creating a multicolor, marbled effect.

EMBELLISHING

With sewing needle threaded with embroidery floss, embellish tops of buttons as desired.

FINISHING BUTTONS

With threaded sewing needle, sew one jump ring to center of flat side of each button. Sew buttons to your favorite sweater, jacket, or bag.

garland

THIS GARLAND COMBINES *knitting, felting, and sewing without a lot of fuss* OR MUSS. BASIC PANELS OF STOCKINETTE STITCH ARE KNITTED AND THEN FELTED. ONCE THE FELTED FABRIC IS DRY, *circles are cut in a variety of sizes* AND THEN SEWN TOGETHER INTO A LONG STRIP. YOU CAN WRAP THE RESULTING STRAND OF COLOR AROUND YOUR HOLIDAY TREE—OR EVEN AROUND YOUR BODY AS A *necklace, scarf, or belt.*

....

FINISHED MEASUREMENTS
KNIT YARDAGE:
21 x 40", before felting
13½ x 19", after felting
Results will depend on felting conditions and time spent felting.

ASSEMBLED GARLAND/SCARF: 119" long

YARN
Malabrigo Yarn Worsted (100% merino; 215 yards / 100 grams): 2 hanks #35 frank ochre

NEEDLES
One 24" circular needle size US 11 (8 mm)
Change needle size if necessary to obtain the correct gauge.

NOTIONS
4" Omnigrid scissors, or small, very sharp scissors
Roll of tracing paper
Straight pins
Metallic sewing thread
Sewing machine

GAUGE
15 sts and 25 rows = 4" (10 cm) in Stockinette stitch (St st)

KNIT YARDAGE
CO 79 sts.
Row 1 (RS): Knit.

Row 2: K2, purl to last 2 sts, k2.
Work Rows 1 and 2 until piece measures 40".

FELTING
Felt knit yardage following instructions in Felting Basics, page 8. Once felted, lay fabric flat and set aside to dry.

FINISHING
From dry, felted fabric, cut the following circles:
A: 18 circles, 2½" in diameter
B: 3 circles, 2½" in diameter with center hole 1½" in diameter
C: 3 circles, 2½" in diameter with center hole 1" in diameter
D: 16 circles, 2" in diameter
E: 14 circles, 1½" in diameter
F: 6 circles, 1" in diameter

Cut length of tracing paper 3 x 119". Beginning at one end of tracing paper, pin circles to paper (this will stabilize circles prior to sewing). With edges of circles touching one another, place circles in order desired, or as follows: 3F, 3E, 1D, 1A, 1B, 1A, 1D, 5A, 1D, 1E, 1D, 1C, 2D, 2A, 1D, 1E, 1D, 2A, 1C, 1D, 1E, 1D, 1E, 1D, 1B, 1A, 1D, 3E, 1D, 3A, 1B, 1A, 1D, 3E, 1D, 1A, 1C, 1A, 1D, 1E, 3F.

With metallic sewing thread and sewing machine, straight-stitch circles together. Gently remove tracing paper backing. Machine-sew an additional straight stitch over the first line of stitching for reinforcement.

ornaments

—— • ——

QUICK AND EASY, *these ornaments all begin as the same basic round shape.* JUST BEFORE FELTING THEY ARE *stuffed with fiberfill,* THEN AFTER FELTING, WHILE STILL WET, *the balls are bound with rubber bands* WHEREVER TIERS ARE DESIRED.

....

FINISHED MEASUREMENTS

3 (4½)" wide x 4 (5)" high, before felting, laid flat
6½ (8)" circumference, after felting and stuffing
Results will depend on felting conditions and time spent felting.

YARN

Malabrigo Yarn Worsted (100% merino; 215 yards / 100 grams): 1 hank makes 4 large and 3 small ornaments, 6 large ornaments, or 13 small ornaments. Shown in #23 pagoda, #609 purple magic, #150 azul profundo, #37 lettuce, #148 hollyhock, #83 water green, #96 sunset, #93 fucsia, #35 frank ochre

NEEDLES

One set of 4 or 5 double-pointed needles (dpn) size
US 10½ (6.5 mm)
Change needle size if necessary to obtain the correct gauge.

NOTIONS

Stitch marker
Tapestry needle
Polyester fiberfill
Digital kitchen scale
Crochet hook size US G/6 (4 mm)
2 or 3 small lingerie bags with zippers
OPTIONAL: small rubber bands, U- or T-pins, binder clips, and embroidery floss
OPTIONAL: size 8 seed beads, sequins, appliqué pins, and Aleene's Tacky Glue

GAUGE

16½ sts and 23 rows = 4" (10 cm) in Stockinette stitch (St st)

SMALL ORNAMENT

CO 8 sts, leaving a 12" tail for later use in sewing bottom seam. Join for working in the rnd, being careful not to twist sts; place marker (pm) for beginning of rnd.

Rnd 1: Knit.
Rnd 2: *K1-f/b; repeat from * to end—16 sts.
Rnds 3-4: Knit.
Rnd 5: *K1, k1-f/b; repeat from * to end—24 sts.
Rnds 6-18: Knit.
Rnd 19: *K1, k2tog, k1, ssk; repeat from * to end—16 sts.
Rnds 20-21: Knit.
Rnd 22: *K2tog, ssk; repeat from * to end—8 sts.
Rnd 23: Knit.

Cut yarn, leaving a 36" tail. Using tapestry needle, thread tail loosely through 8 remaining sts. Leave opening large enough to stuff ornament.

LARGE ORNAMENT

CO 12 sts, leaving a 12" tail for later use in sewing bottom seam. Join for working in the rnd, being careful not to twist sts; pm for beginning of rnd.

Rnds 1-2: Knit.

Rnd 3: *K1-f/b; repeat from * to end—24 sts.

Rnds 4-6: Knit.

Rnd 7: *K1, k1-f/b; repeat from * to end—36 sts.

Rnds 8-24: Knit.

Rnd 25: *K1, k2tog, k1, ssk; repeat from * to end—24 sts.

Rnds 26-27: Knit.

Rnd 28: *K2tog, ssk; repeat from * to end—12 sts.

Rnd 29: Knit.

Cut yarn, leaving a 40" tail. Using tapestry needle, thread tail loosely through 12 remaining sts. Leave opening large enough to stuff ornament.

FINISHING

Using tapestry needle threaded with cast-on tail, sew bottom seam of ornament.

Stuff knit ornament with polyester fiberfill through opening at top. Place on digital scale—ornament should weigh approximately .30 (.55) oz.

Be careful not to overstuff your ornaments. If you overstuff them, the fiberfill will constrict the knit fabric and prevent areas from felting. Resist the temptation to stuff your ornaments with wool fleece instead of the recommended polyester fiberfill. Wool fleece felts at a much different rate than your knitting; using it results in very small centers for your ornaments (similar to a clapper inside a bell) and an uneven surface.

Pull tail at top of ornament snug to close opening. Using crochet hook, work chain st for 7 (9)" (see Special Techniques, page 129). Fasten off by drawing end of tail through last loop formed. Using tapestry needle, secure end to base of chain, forming a loop at top of ornament.

FELTING

Place one or two ornaments in each lingerie bag. Felt ornaments following instructions in Felting Basics, page 8.

Note #2

You can felt the ornaments without the lingerie bags, but keep a very close eye on the ornaments as they felt. The loops at the top of your ornaments tend to tangle and twist together at the beginning of the felting process. Using the lingerie bags helps keep the ornaments separate and ensures each piece felts correctly.

Once ornaments are felted and rinsed with cold water, roll each ornament in your hands to refine its round shape, if needed. If a tiered shape is desired, wrap rubber bands around wet ornament at desired locations.

Note #3

If your felted fabric puckers when wrapped with rubber bands, it's not sufficiently felted. For a smooth surface, continue felting until the ornament is firm, then wrap with rubber bands.

Rubber bands wrapped close to the bottom of the ornament may need to be secured with U- or T-pins. Pins can also be used to maintain the shape of your tiered ornament while it dries.

Binder clips can be used at the bottom of your ornament to create more of a flat edge. Slip a small piece of fabric or bubble wrap between your ornament and the clip to prevent the clip from leaving an indentation on your ornament.

Place ornaments on drying rack and allow to air-dry. Once ornaments are dry, remove rubber bands, pins, and clips.

EMBELLISHMENT *(optional)*

Slip seed bead and/or sequin onto stem of appliqué pin. Dab pointed tip of pin in glue and push pin into surface of ornament at desired location. Repeat as desired.

For tiered ornaments, cut approximately 8 to 10" length of embroidery floss and wrap around ornament at indentation. Thread ends onto tapestry needle and push through center of ornament, burying ends into fiberfill center.

christmas stockings

—— • • ——

WHILE *I'll always feel nostalgic about the Christmas stocking* OF MY YOUTH, WHICH I STILL HANG ON THE MANTLE EVERY DECEMBER, I COULDN'T RESIST THE TEMPTATION TO PLAY WITH TRADITION A BIT AND CREATE THESE *whimsical Suess-like variations.* UNFELTED AND WORN UPSIDE DOWN, *they also make jolly stocking caps.*

....

FINISHED MEASUREMENTS

29 (35½)" long from top of folded cuff to base of I-cord curl, before felting
23 (27)" long from top of folded cuff to base of I-cord curl, after felting
Results will depend on felting conditions and time spent felting.

YARN

Malabrigo Yarn Worsted (100% merino; 215 yards / 100 grams):
1 (2) hanks MC, 1 hank A, and optionally 1 hank B for striped version.
Small solid stocking shown in #35 frank ochre (MC) and #135 emerald (A).
Large solid stocking shown in #148 hollyhock (MC) and #37 lettuce (A).
Small striped stocking shown in #23 pagoda (MC), #609 purple magic (A), and #37 lettuce (B).
Large striped stocking shown in #135 emerald (MC), #35 frank ochre (A), and #23 pagoda (B).

NEEDLES

One 16" circular needle size US 8 (5 mm)
One 16" circular needle size US 10½ (6.5 mm)
One set of 5 double-pointed needles (dpn) size US 10½ (6.5 mm)
Change needle size if necessary to obtain the correct gauge.

NOTIONS

Stitch marker, tapestry needle, plastic grocery bags, straight pins

GAUGE

17 sts and 23 rows = 4" (10 cm) in Stockinette stitch (St st) using larger needles

Note #1

To avoid creating jogs at color changes, work a "jogless jog" at each color change as follows: Work 1 rnd (either knit or purl, as directed) in new color. Remove marker. Insert tip of right needle into st of old color below left needle, and work together with first st of new color. Replace marker—beginning of rnds moved 1 st to left.

STOCKING

CUFF: With smaller circular needle and A, CO 61 (83) sts. Join for working in the rnd, being careful not to twist sts; place marker (pm) for beginning of rnd. Purl 1 rnd. Knit 1 rnd. Work even in Rev St st (purl all rnds) until cuff measures 1½ (2)" from CO edge.

Increase 3 (5) sts evenly on next rnd—64 (88) sts. Change to larger circular needle and work even in Rev St st until cuff measures 5 (7)" from CO edge.

BODY: Knit 1 rnd. Change to MC and purl 3 rnds. Change to St st and work even until leg measures 12 (9)" from beginning of MC, working all rnds in MC (for solid version) or alternating 11 rnds MC and 3 rnds B (for striped version).

Continuing in MC or stripe sequence, shape stocking as follows:

LARGE SIZE ONLY:
*K9, k2tog; repeat from * to end—80 sts.
Work 17 rnds even.
*K8, k2tog; repeat from * to end—72 sts.
Work 17 rnds even.
*K7, k2tog; repeat from * to end—64 sts.
Work 17 rnds even.

BOTH SIZES:
*K6, k2tog; repeat from * to end—56 sts.
Work 17 rnds even.
*K6, k2tog; repeat from * to end—49 sts.
Work 17 rnds even.
*K5, k2tog; repeat from * to end—42 sts.
Work 15 rnds even.
*K4, k2tog; repeat from * to end—35 sts.
Work 13 rnds even.
*K3, k2tog; repeat from * to end—28 sts.
Work 11 rnds even.
*K2, k2tog; repeat from * to end—21 sts.
Work 9 rnds even.
*K1, k2tog; repeat from * to end—14 sts.
Work 5 rnds even.
*K2tog; repeat from * to end—7 sts.

I-CORD CURL (optional): Knit 7 remaining sts onto 1 dpn. Work 7-st I-cord for 6 (8)" (see Special Techniques, page 129).

FINISHING
Cut yarn, leaving 6" tail. Using tapestry needle, thread tail through 7 remaining sts. Weave in loose end.

LOOP: Fold cuff over so RS of St st is facing you. With dpn and choice of color, pick up and knit 6 sts from last row of A. Work 6-st I-Cord for 9". BO. Cut yarn, leaving 6" tail. Using tapestry needle and tail, sew BO edge to base of I-Cord to form loop.

FELTING
Unfold cuff and place stocking in washing machine. Felt stocking following instructions in Felting Basics, page 8.

Note #2

Check felting progress approximately every 3 to 4 minutes. If narrow shape at bottom of stocking begins to crease, remove stocking from machine (you may need a pair of dishwashing gloves—remember, the water is hot!) and reposition knitting so that no creases are forming as the stocking felts. Return stocking to machine and continue felting, checking frequently, until stocking is fully felted.

Once stocking is fully felted, remove from machine. Fold cuff over and shape stocking. Stuff stocking with plastic grocery bags to help stocking maintain desired shape. Coil optional I-Cord curl into desired shape and secure with straight pin. Allow stocking to dry fully. Remove plastic bags and straight pin.

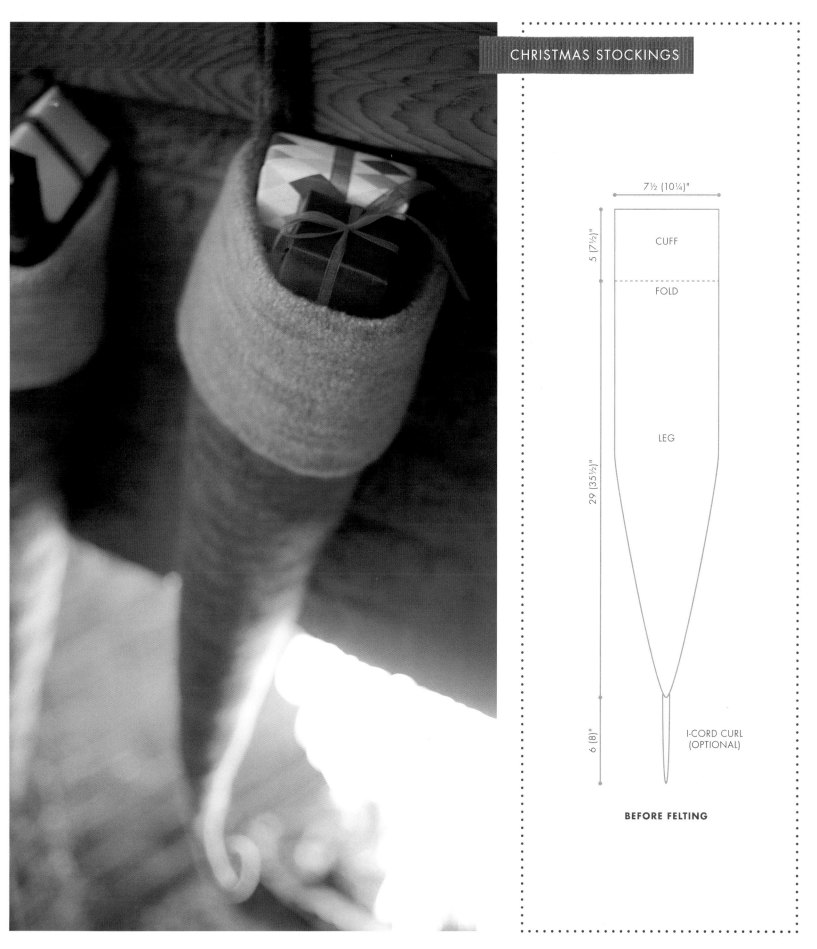

7½ (10¼)"

5 (7½)"

CUFF

FOLD

LEG

29 (35½)"

I-CORD CURL
(OPTIONAL)

6 (8)"

BEFORE FELTING

christmas tree skirt

—•—

IF YOU THINK THIS TREE SKIRT LOOKS COMPLICATED TO MAKE, *look again* BECAUSE BUT IT'S ACTUALLY QUITE SIMPLE—*it doesn't even require any sewing.* FIRST YOU KNIT AND FELT PANELS OF STOCKINETTE-STITCH FABRIC, THEN YOU *cut out circles in a variety of sizes,* THEN YOU ATTACH THEM TO A WOOL BACKING FABRIC USING DOUBLE-SIDED FUSIBLE INTERFACING. IF DESIRED, AS A FINAL FLOURISH, YOU CAN *add embroidery to random circles (perhaps a few each Christmas* INSTEAD OF ALL AT THE SAME TIME). THIS SKIRT CAN ALSO BE MADE OUT OF *circles cut from felted wool sweaters* OR WOVEN WOOL FABRIC.

....

FINISHED MEASUREMENTS

KNIT YARDAGE:

21 x 40", before felting

15 x 21", after felting

Results will depend on felting conditions and time spent felting.

TREE SKIRT:

55" diameter, after assembly

YARN

Malabrigo Yarn Worsted (100% merino; 215 yards / 100 grams): 24 hanks #41 burgundy

NEEDLES

One 24" circular needle size US 11 (8 mm)

Change needle size if necessary to obtain the correct gauge.

NOTIONS

2 sheets 36 x 55" butcher paper

Tape

Pencil

Tape measure or yardstick

Straight pins

4" Omnigrid scissors or small, very sharp scissors

3¾ yards 12" wide Steam-A-Seam 2 double-sided fusible web

Steam iron

1⅝ yards 55" wide wool fabric

Fabric scissors

OPTIONAL: embroidery needle and 10 skeins DMC rayon embroidery floss color #30814

GAUGE

15 sts and 25 rows = 4" (10 cm) in Stockinette stitch (St st)

KNIT YARDAGE *(make 12)*

CO 79 sts.

Row 1 (RS): Knit.

Row 2: K2, purl to last 2 sts, k2.

Work Rows 1 and 2 until piece measures 40".

Note #1

A piece of yardage measuring 21 x 40" will require approximately 2 hanks of yarn. I found this size to be small enough to manage easily during the felting process, and large enough that, once felted, it yields many cut circles with a minimum of waste.

FELTING

Felt knit yardage following instructions in Felting Basics, page 8. Smooth pieces out as much as possible (flat pieces such as these tend to flare a bit once felted) and set aside to dry.

Note #2

Plan to felt your knit yardage in batches. Depending on the size of your washing machine, you should be able to felt 3 to 4 panels at the same time. Make sure your fabric has enough room to move freely; don't overload your machine such that your knitting is constricted while felting.

PAPER TEMPLATES

Tape 2 pieces of butcher paper together. Cut to measure 55" square. Fold in half horizontally and then vertically. Mark center point with pencil, then unfold. Draw circle 55" in diameter by measuring 27½" out from center point and marking with pencil at 1" intervals around the circle. Cut along marks to create circle 55" in diameter. Draw a second circle 16" in diameter by measuring 8" out from center of first circle. Cut out center opening. Draw dotted line along 1 fold line from center opening to outside edge to indicate cut line for back opening of skirt. Opposite cut line, mark center front of skirt.

From remaining butcher paper, cut 3 or 4 circle templates in each of the following sizes: 6, 3½, 3, 2, and 1¾" in diameter.

CIRCLES

Pin circle templates onto dry, felted fabric, abutting templates with fabric edges and each other to get the maximum number of circles from each piece of felted fabric. Arrange the larger circles first, so that their remnants can be used for the smaller circles. Using scissors, cut the following number of circles from felted fabric, and corresponding pieces of fusible web:

23 circles, 6" in diameter, and 23 pieces of fusible web 2¾" square
94 circles, 3½" in diameter, and 94 pieces of fusible web 1½" square
19 circles, 3" in diameter, and 19 pieces of fusible web 1¼" square
51 circles, 2" in diameter, and 51 pieces of fusible web ¾" square
70 circles, 1¾" in diameter, and 70 pieces of fusible web ½" square

Note #3

I found that a 4" pair of sharp scissors was the best for getting a nice clean edge and made the circles easy to cut out.

BACKING FABRIC

Fold wool backing fabric in half. Fold paper template in half along cut line. Place paper template on top of fabric, aligning folds. Pin paper template into place. Using fabric scissors, cut backing fabric as indicated by paper template. Mark center front of skirt with straight pin.

ASSEMBLY

For each circle, remove paper backing from one side of corresponding piece of fusible web, and stick to wrong side of circle.

Lay backing fabric flat on table or floor. Arrange circles as shown in diagram, beginning with 3½" circles at outer edges and working from center front towards back. Remove paper backing and stick circles to backing fabric. Secure with straight pins.

Following directions provided with fusible web, iron to fuse circles to backing fabric, being careful not to iron over pins (many decorative pin tops melt when ironed). Use bursts of steam to adhere circles to backing fabric. Let tree skirt cool (as it cools, the circles will become more secure).

EMBELLISHMENT *(optional)*

With embroidery needle threaded with a full strand of floss, work running stitch around perimeter of random circles.

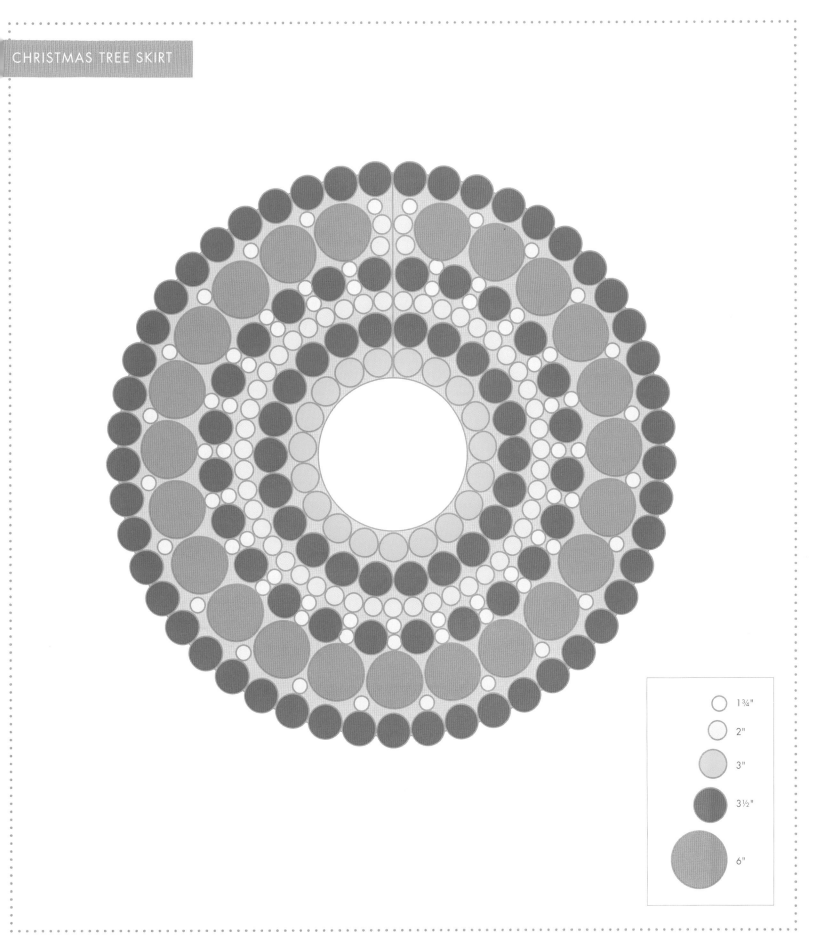

1¾"

2"

3"

3½"

6"

full circle purse

The circle is one of my favorite shapes. IT'S PLEASING TO LOOK AT AND, FOR ME, IT SYMBOLICALLY REPRESENTS THE IDEA OF COMING TO A RESOLUTION. HOWEVER, TO CREATE THIS CIRCULAR PURSE VIA FELTING, YOU HAVE TO first knit an oval. THIS IS BECAUSE knit stitches are not equal IN HEIGHT AND WIDTH AND SO KNITTED FABRIC DOESN'T NOT SHRINK PROPORTIONALLY. THE alpaca-silk blend WITH WHICH I MADE THIS PURSE GIVES IT A smooth texture with an appealing sheen.

FINISHED MEASUREMENTS
13¼ x 15½", before felting
10" diameter, after felting
Results will depend on felting conditions and time spent felting.

YARN
Misti Alpaca Suri Silk (80% baby suri alpaca, 20% silk;
109 yards / 50 grams): 2 skeins. Shown in RJ2110 coral

NEEDLES
One set of 5 double-pointed needles (dpn) size US 8 (5 mm)
One 16" circular needle size US 8 (5 mm)
Change needle size if necessary to obtain the correct gauge.

NOTIONS
Stitch markers
Stitch holder or waste yarn
Tapestry needle
Smooth cotton waste yarn, for basting
OPTIONAL: ⅓ yard fabric, dressmaker's pencil, fabric scissors, iron, and sewing machine, pins, needle, and thread, for lining
OPTIONAL: ½" or ¾" magnetic bag closure

GAUGE
20 sts and 25 rows = 4" (10 cm) in Stockinette stitch (St st)

Note #1

Bag is knit in Stockinette stitch, then felted with either the Stockinette or the Reverse Stockinette side of the fabric on the outside of the bag. Coral bag is shown with Stockinette on outside.

BAG
CO 56 sts. Divide sts evenly on dpns. Join for working in the rnd, placing markers at beginning of rnd and after 28th st. Work in St st for 4 rnds. Shape bag as follows, changing to circular needle as desired:

Increase Rnd 1: K1, [k1-f/b] 3 times, knit to 4 sts before next marker, [k1-f/b] 3 times, k1, slip marker (sm), k1, [k1-f/b] 3 times, knit to 4 sts before end-of-rnd marker, [k1-f/b] 3 times, k1—68 sts.
Work 2 rnds even.
Repeat last 3 rnds twice—92 sts.

Increase Rnd 2: K1, [k1-f/b] twice, knit to 3 sts before marker, [k1-f/b] twice, k1, sm, k1, [k1-f/b] twice, knit to 3 sts before end-of-rnd marker, [k1-f/b] twice, k1—100 sts.
Work 3 rnds even.
Repeat last 4 rnds 4 times—132 sts.
Work even for 6".

Decrease Rnd 1: K1, [ssk] twice, knit to 5 sts before next marker, [k2tog] twice, k1, sm, k1, [ssk] twice, knit to 5 sts before end-of-rnd marker, [k2tog] twice, k1—124 sts.
Work 3 rnds even.
Repeat last 4 rnds once, then work Decrease Rnd 1 once more—108 sts.

SIDE ONE

Remove beginning-of-rnd marker, k54 to next marker. Remove marker, and slip next 54 sts to st holder or waste yarn. Turn and work 3 rows of St st, beginning with a purl row. Shape top as follows:

Decrease Row 1 (RS): Slip 1, [ssk] twice, knit to last 5 sts, [k2tog] twice, k1—50 sts. Working in St st, work 3 rows even.
Repeat last 4 rows once—46 sts.

Decrease Row 2 (RS): Slip 1, [ssk] 3 times, knit to last 7 sts, [k2tog] 3 times, k1—40 sts. Work 1 row even.
Repeat Decrease Row 2 once—34 sts.

Next Row: P8, BO center 18 sts to create handle opening, purl to end of row—16 sts.
Next Row: K1, ssk, k5, CO 16 sts, k5, k2tog, k1—30 sts.

Decrease Row 3 (WS): P1, p2tog, purl to last 3 sts, p2tog, p1—28 sts.

Decrease Row 4 (RS): K1, [ssk] twice, knit to last 5 sts, [k2tog] twice, k1—24 sts. Work 2 rows even.

Decrease Row 5 (WS): P1, [p2tog] 3 times, purl to end of row—21 sts.

Decrease Row 6 (RS): K1, [k2tog] 3 times, knit to end of row—18 sts.

BO all sts.

SIDE TWO

Slip sts from st holder or waste yarn back onto needles. With RS of Side Two facing you, join yarn at right edge. Work 4 rows of St st, beginning with a RS knit row. Shape top as for Side One.

FINISHING

Determine if you want St st or Rev St st on outside of bag. With yarn threaded onto tapestry needle, sew bottom seam. Weave in loose ends. With cotton waste yarn threaded onto tapestry needle, loosely baste open portions of bag closed, along both upper edge and handle openings.

Note #2

Loosely basting the openings closed keeps the openings from flaring during the felting process. Keep a very close eye on this section while felting—overfelting may cause it to felt together. If this area begins to felt together, gently pull the bag open.

FELTING

Felt bag following instructions in Felting Basics, page 8. Allow bag to dry completely, then remove cotton basting thread by gently pulling on one end.

LINING AND MAGNETIC CLOSURE (optional)

ASSEMBLE LINING: Fold lining fabric in half, and place felted bag on top. With dressmaker's pencil, trace shape of bag onto fabric. Cut through both layers of fabric to create 2 pieces. Trim top portion of each piece, as shown in Step 1. With RS's together, machine-stitch lining pieces together around perimeter, beginning and ending 1½" below trimmed tops, as shown in Step 2. Fold raw fabric edges at top and sides of lining to WS by ¼", and press with warm iron.

ATTACH MAGNETIC CLOSURE: Mark placement of first half of magnetic closure on one side of lining, centered horizontally and located approximately ½" below top of lining. Using closure as guide, make two ¼" cuts into fabric for closure prongs. On RS of fabric, insert closure prongs into cuts. On WS of fabric, slip flat disc (companion piece to closure half) over prongs. Press down on prongs, securing closure half in place. Repeat with second half of closure on opposite side of lining.

INSERT LINING: Slip lining into felted bag with WS of lining facing WS of bag, and pin lining into place. With sewing needle, sew lining in place.

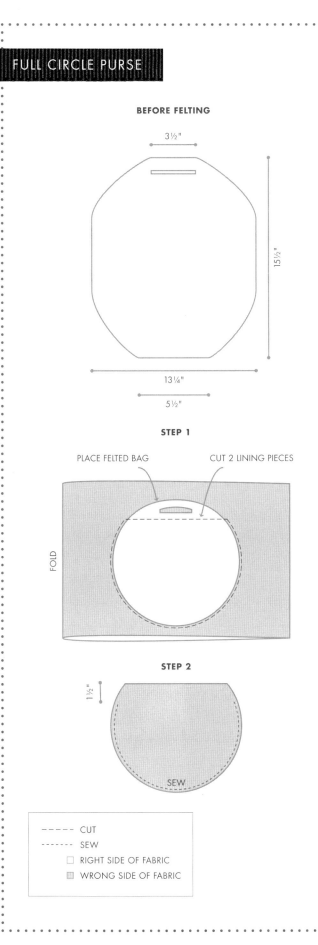

BEFORE FELTING

3½"

15½"

13¼"

5½"

STEP 1

PLACE FELTED BAG

CUT 2 LINING PIECES

FOLD

STEP 2

1½"

SEW

- - - - - CUT
- - - - - SEW
☐ RIGHT SIDE OF FABRIC
▨ WRONG SIDE OF FABRIC

hazel & maude pot holders

— • —

I was thinking about my two grandmothers WHILE I WAS DESIGNING THESE POT HOLDERS. MY PATERNAL GRANDMOTHER, MAUDE, *taught me to bake* AND LIKED EVERYTHING VERY NEAT AND ORDERLY. MY MATERNAL GRANDMOTHER, HAZEL, *taught me to sew without a pattern,* AND WHEN I WAS OLD ENOUGH, *to mix a mean martini.*

....

FINISHED MEASUREMENTS
MAUDE (patterned allover): 9¾ x 12¾", before felting, including attached I-Cord trim
HAZEL (patterned halfway): 9¾ x 13½", before felting, including attached I-Cord trim
BOTH: 8½ x 8½", after felting
Results will depend on felting conditions and time spent felting.

YARN
Louet Riverstone Chunky (100% wool; 165 yards / 100 grams):
1 hank each of 4 colors
Colorway One (see left) : #17 shamrock (A), #62 citrus (B), #49 charcoal (C), #26 crabapple (D)
Colorway Two (see page 115): #57 French blue (A), #48 aqua (B), #58 burgundy (C), #35 mustard (D)

NEEDLES
One pair straight needles size US 11 (8 mm)
Two double-pointed needles (dpn) size US 11 (8 mm)
Change needle size if necessary to obtain the correct gauge.

NOTIONS
Tapestry needle

GAUGE
13 sts and 17 rows = 4" (10 cm) in Stockinette stitch (St st)
13 sts and 24 rows = 4" (10 cm) in Blister stitch

Note
If substituting other yarns, avoid those containing mohair or llama. These fibers usually create a "fuzzy" felted fabric that isn't desirable for use around food and is also more flammable.

The Blister st used here is adapted from the Four-Color Blister Stitch in *A Second Treasury of Knitting Patterns* by Barbara G. Walker.

MAUDE
Using A, CO 29 sts and purl one WS row. Carrying A along selvedge, and cutting and rejoining B, C, and D as necessary, work in Blister st as follows:

Rows 1, 3, and 5 (RS): Using B, knit.
Rows 2, 4, and 6: Using B, purl.
Row 7: Using A, k4, *drop next st off needle and unravel 6 rows down, insert needle from front into color A st in 7th row below and knit (catching the 6 loose strands in st), k3, repeat from * to last st, k1.
Row 8: Using A, purl.
Rows 9-14: Using C, repeat Rows 1-6.
Row 15: Using A, k2, *drop next st off needle and unravel 6 rows down, insert needle from front into color A st in 7th row below and knit (catching the 6 loose strands in st), k3, repeat from *, end last repeat with k2 instead of k3.
Row 16: Using A, purl.

Rows 17-22: Using D, repeat Rows 1-6.

Rows 23-24: Repeat Rows 7-8.

Rows 25-30: Using B, repeat Rows 1-6.

Rows 31-32: Repeat Rows 15-16.

Rows 33-38: Using C, repeat Rows 1-6.

Rows 39-40: Repeat Rows 7-8.

Rows 41-46: Using D, repeat Rows 1-6.

Rows 47-48: Repeat Rows 15-16.

Rows 49-54: Using B, repeat Rows 1-6.

Rows 55-56: Repeat Rows 7-8.

Rows 57-62: Using C, repeat Rows 1-6.

Rows 63-64: Repeat Rows 15-16.

Rows 65-70: Using D, repeat Rows 1-6.

Row 71: Repeat Row 7.

Cut yarn, leaving 4" tail. Proceed to FINISHING instructions.

HAZEL

Using A, CO 29 sts and purl one WS row. Carrying A and B along selvedge, work in Blister st as follows:

Rows 1, 3, and 5 (RS): Using B, knit.

Rows 2, 4, and 6: Using B, purl.

Row 7: Using A, k4, *drop next st off needle and unravel 6 rows down, insert needle from front into color A st in 7th row below and knit (catching the 6 loose strands in st), k3, repeat from * to last st, k1.

Row 8: Using A, purl.

Rows 9-14: Repeat Rows 1-6.

Row 15: Using A, k2, *drop next st off needle and unravel 6 rows down, insert needle from front into color A st in 7th row below and knit (catching the 6 loose strands in st), k3, repeat from *, end last repeat with k2 instead of k3.

Row 16: Using A, purl.

Rows 17-22: Repeat Rows 1-6.

Rows 23-24: Repeat Rows 7-8.

Rows 25-30: Repeat Rows 1-6.

Rows 31-32: Repeat Rows 15-16.

FOR COLORWAY ONE: Using C, knit one RS row, increasing 5 sts evenly—34 sts. Work 2 more rows in St st. Change to D, and work even in St st until pot holder measures 13½" from CO edge. Cut yarn, leaving 4" tail.

FOR COLORWAY TWO: Using D, knit one RS row, increasing 5 sts evenly—34 sts. Work 2 more rows in St st. Change to C, and work even in St st until pot holder measures 13½" from CO edge. Cut yarn, leaving 4" tail.

FINISHING

WORK I-CORD TRIM: Using new strand of A and empty dpn, CO 3 sts for I-Cord. With WS of pot holder facing you, work I-Cord BO across 29 pot holder sts as follows: *[K2, slip 1] across I-Cord sts, knit 1 pot holder st, psso. Slide I-Cord sts to right end of dpn. Repeat from * to top corner.

MAKE HANGING LOOP: At top corner, work I-Cord for 8" (see Special Techniques, page 129). Close loop as follows: K2, slip 1, pick up and knit 1 st from last st of I-Cord BO, psso. Slide sts to right end of dpn.

CONTINUE TRIM: Work attached I-Cord to bottom corner of pot holder as follows: *K2, slip 1, pick up and knit 1 st from edge of pot holder, psso, slide sts to right end of dpn, repeat from * to bottom corner.

TURN CORNER: At bottom corner, k3, do not pick up a st along side edge, slide sts to right end of dpn. K2, slip 1, pick up and knit 1 st from corner, psso, slide sts to right end of dpn. K3, do not pick up a st along bottom edge, slide sts to right end of dpn.

Continue working attached I-Cord and turning corners around remainder of pot holder. BO all sts. Sew ends of I-Cord together. If necessary, close gap at base of hanging loop with strand of A threaded on tapestry needle. Weave in loose ends.

FELTING

Felt pot holders following instructions in Felting Basics, page 8.

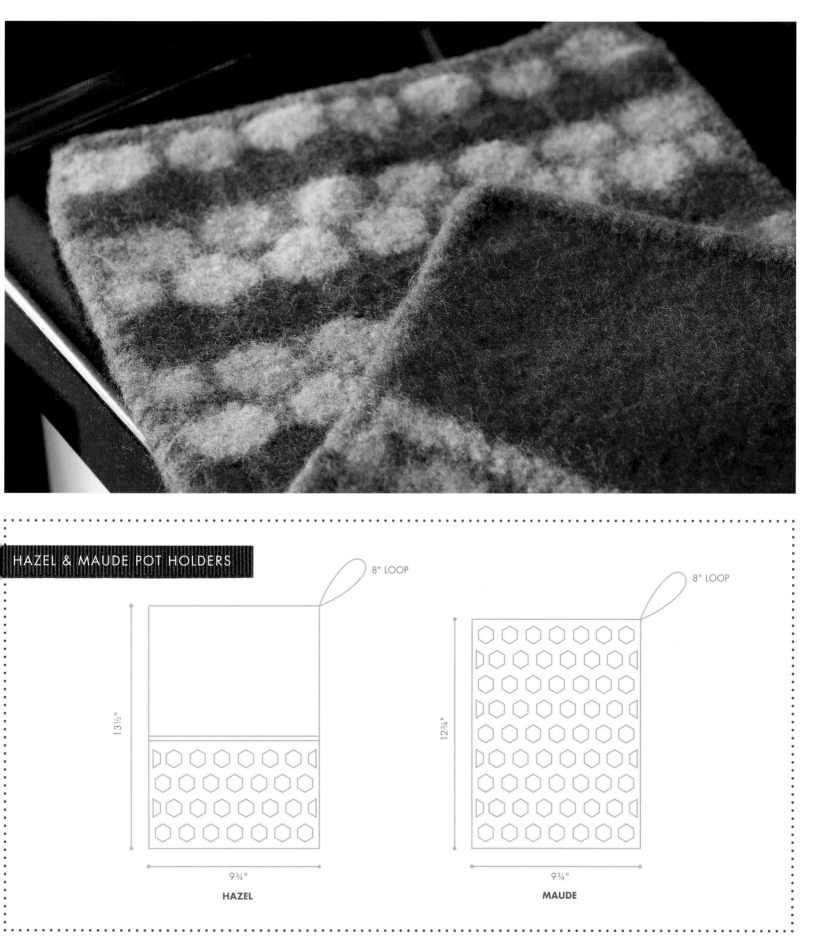

HAZEL & MAUDE POT HOLDERS

8" LOOP

13½"

9¾"

HAZEL

8" LOOP

12¾"

9¾"

MAUDE

oversized carry-all

THIS IS ONE OF *my favorite bags for traveling.* EVERYTHING I NEED FOR A SHORT TRIP USUALLY FITS INSIDE, IT'S *easy to squeeze into an airplane's overhead compartment,* AND IT HAS COME IN *handy as a pillow* MORE THAN ONCE WHEN I'VE NEEDED TO NAP IN TRANSIT.

FINISHED MEASUREMENTS
36½ x 30¾" body with 31" handle, before felting, with work unassembled and laid flat
27 x 19" body with 22" handle, after felting
Results will depend on felting conditions and time spent felting.

YARN
Louet Riverstone Chunky (100% wool; 165 yards / 100 grams): 8 hanks #42 eggplant (A); 1 hank each #48 aqua (B), #35 mustard (C), #53 caribou (D), #55 willow (E), #58 burgundy (F)

NEEDLES
One 29" to 36" circular needle size US 10½ (6.5 mm)
Two double-pointed needles (dpn) size US 10½ (6.5 mm)
Change needle size if necessary to obtain the correct gauge.

NOTIONS
Stitch holder or waste yarn
Tapestry needle

GAUGE
12½ sts and 19 rows = 4" (10 cm) in Stockinette stitch (St st)

POCKETS *(make 2)*
Using A, CO 19 sts. Work in St st for 13". Slip sts onto st holder or waste yarn.

BAG
Using A, CO 228 sts. Join for working in the rnd, being careful not to twist sts; pm for beginning of rnd. Knit first round, placing markers after 95th, 114th, and 209th sts (95 sts between markers for front and for back, 19 sts for each side gusset). Work even in St st until work measures 17½".

POCKET PLACEMENT: Knit to first marker, remove marker, BO 19 sts at first side gusset, remove next marker. Knit to next marker, remove marker, and BO 19 sts at second side gusset; leave marker at end of rnd in place.

Next Rnd: K95, position first pocket inside bag and knit across 19 sts of first pocket, k95, position second pocket inside bag and knit across 19 sts of second pocket.

Using A, knit 1 rnd even. Continuing in St st, work the following color sequence twice: 3 rnds B, 3C, 2D, 6E, 2D, 4F, 2A, 2D, 3E, 3A. Continuing with A, BO all sts.

FINISHING
Using tapestry needle threaded with A and mattress stitch, sew bottom seam (see Special Techniques, page 129). Turn bag inside out and flatten bottom as shown in diagram. Sew a short seam across triangular flap at each side approximately 3½" from end of each triangle point, to form bottom and side gussets. Sew sides and bottom of each pocket to inside of bag using whip stitch (see Special Techniques, page 129), being careful that seaming yarn does not show through to the RS of fabric. Weave in loose ends. Turn bag RS out.

HANDLES *(make 2)*

Lay bag flat and mark top of bag 8" from right edge for beginning of handle, and 8" from left edge for end of handle. Using a dpn, pick up 7 handle sts starting at beginning marker and working towards center of bag. Using 2 dpns, and holding together 2 strands of A, work as follows until handle measures 31": *K4, bring yarn forward, slip 3, turn; repeat from * to end. BO all sts, leaving 10" tails. Using tapestry needle threaded with tails, sew end of handle to same side of bag at marked position.

Turn bag over and repeat for second handle, on opposite side of bag.

FELTING

Felt bag following the instructions in Felting Basics, page 8.

OVERSIZED CARRY-ALL

- - - - - - - SEW
☐ RIGHT SIDE OF FABRIC
▥ WRONG SIDE OF FABRIC

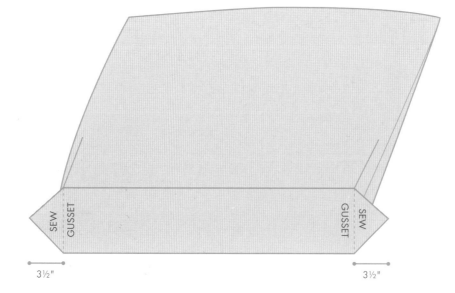

wool nesting boxes

—— • ——

THESE *boxes are knitted in the round in a tube shape* WITH FOUR COLUMNS OF EVENLY SPACED YARNOVERS, THEN FELTED AND MOLDED INTO SHAPE. *We're it not for yarnovers,* WHICH CREATE "HINGES" AT THE FOUR CORNERS, *these boxes would be bowls.*

....

FINISHED MEASUREMENTS
2¼ (3¾, 5¼)" wide x 3 (5, 7½)" high, before felting
2 (3¼, 4½)" square, after felting
Results will depend on felting conditions and time spent felting.

YARN
Manos del Uruguay Wool (100% wool; 135 yards / 100 grams): 2 hanks (makes one box in each size). Shown in #57 raspberry, #X topaz, and #E English.

NEEDLES
One set of 5 double-pointed needles (dpn) size US 9 (5.5 mm)
Change needle size if necessary to obtain the correct gauge.

NOTIONS
Stitch marker
Tapestry needle

GAUGE
17 sts and 23 rows = 4" (10 cm) in Stockinette stitch (St st)

BOX
CO 40 (64, 88) sts. Join for working in the rnd, being careful not to twist sts; place marker (pm) for beginning of rnd.
Rnds 1 and 3: Purl.
Rnds 2 and 4: *K8 (14, 20), k2tog, yo; repeat from * to end.
Rnd 5: Knit.
Repeat Rnds 2 and 5 until work measures 3 (5, 7½)".

BOTTOM SHAPING
ALL SIZES: Rnd 1: *Sl1-k1-psso, k6 (12, 18), k2tog; repeat

from *—32 (56, 80) sts.
Rnds 2, 4, and 6: Knit.
Rnd 3: *Sl1-k1-psso, k4 (10, 16), k2tog; repeat from *—24 (48, 72) sts.
Rnd 5: *Sl1-k1-psso, k2 (8, 14), k2tog; repeat from *—16 (40, 64) sts.
Rnd 7: *Sl1-k1-psso, k0 (6, 12), k2tog; repeat from *—8 (32, 56) sts.

MEDIUM SIZE ONLY: Rnd 8: Knit.
Rnd 9: *Sl1-k1-psso, k4, k2tog; repeat from *—24 sts.
Rnd 10: *Sl1-k1-psso, k2, k2tog; repeat from *—16 sts.
Rnd 11: *Sl1-k1-psso, k2tog; repeat from *—8 sts.

LARGE SIZE ONLY: Rnds 8, 10, and 12: Knit.
Rnd 9: *Sl1-k1-psso, k10, k2tog; repeat from *—48 sts.
Rnd 11: *Sl1-k1-psso, k8, k2tog; repeat from *—40 sts.
Rnd 13: *Sl1-k1-psso, k6, k2tog; repeat from *—32 sts.
Rnd 14: *Sl1-k1-psso, k4, k2tog; repeat from *—24 sts.
Rnd 15: *Sl1-k1-psso, k2, k2tog; repeat from *—16 sts.
Rnd 16: *Sl1-k1-psso, k2tog; repeat from *—8 sts.

ALL SIZES
Cut yarn, leaving 5" tail. Using tapestry needle, thread tail through 8 remaining sts and pull snug. Bring tail to WS. Weave in loose ends.

FELTING
Felt boxes following instructions in Felting Basics, page 8.

Note

You may find that you need to felt these boxes longer than expected to make them sturdy.

ottoman upholstery

———•———

I love putting knitting in unexpected places. FOR THIS BASIC BOX-SHAPED OTTOMAN, I MADE MY OWN UPHOLSTERY BY KNITTING *textured panels, sewing them together,* AND THEN *felting the whole piece.*

....

FINISHED MEASUREMENTS

22" square and 15" deep, before felting
21½" square and 13" deep, after felting
Results will depend on felting conditions and time spent felting.

YARN

Morehouse Merino 3-Strand Yarn (100% merino wool; 140 yards / 2 ounces): 13 skeins chartreuse

NEEDLES

One 29" circular needle size US 9 (5.5 mm)
Change needle size if necessary to obtain the correct gauge.

NOTIONS

Cable needle (cn)
Tapestry needle
1 Klippan ottoman from IKEA

GAUGE

21 sts and 25 rows = 4" (10 cm) in wave cable portion of Side Chart
18 sts and 24 rows = 4" (10 cm) in Stockinette stitch (St st)

SIDE PANELS *(make 4)*

CO 122 sts. Follow rows 1-107 of Side Chart.

For larger charts in PDF form, which can be printed out at a copy shop, go to leighradford.com.

BO all sts. Finished panel should measure approximately 22 x 15".

TOP *(make 1)*

CO 122 sts. Follow Rows 1-156 of Top Chart. BO all sts. Finished top should measure approximately 22 x 22".

FINISHING

With yarn threaded onto tapestry needle, sew side panels together. (You can choose to have all four panels positioned the same way, or turn one or more of the panels upside-down.) Sew top to side panels. Weave in loose ends.

FELTING

Felt ottoman sleeve following instructions in Felting Basics, page 8.

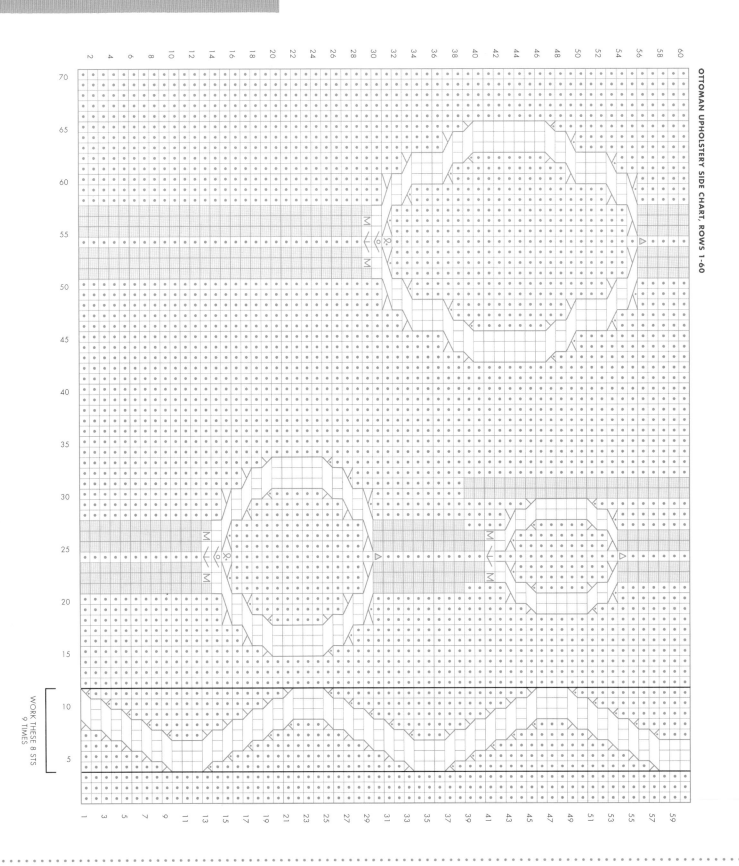

OTTOMAN UPHOLSTERY SIDE CHART, ROWS 1–60

WORK THESE 8 STS
9 TIMES

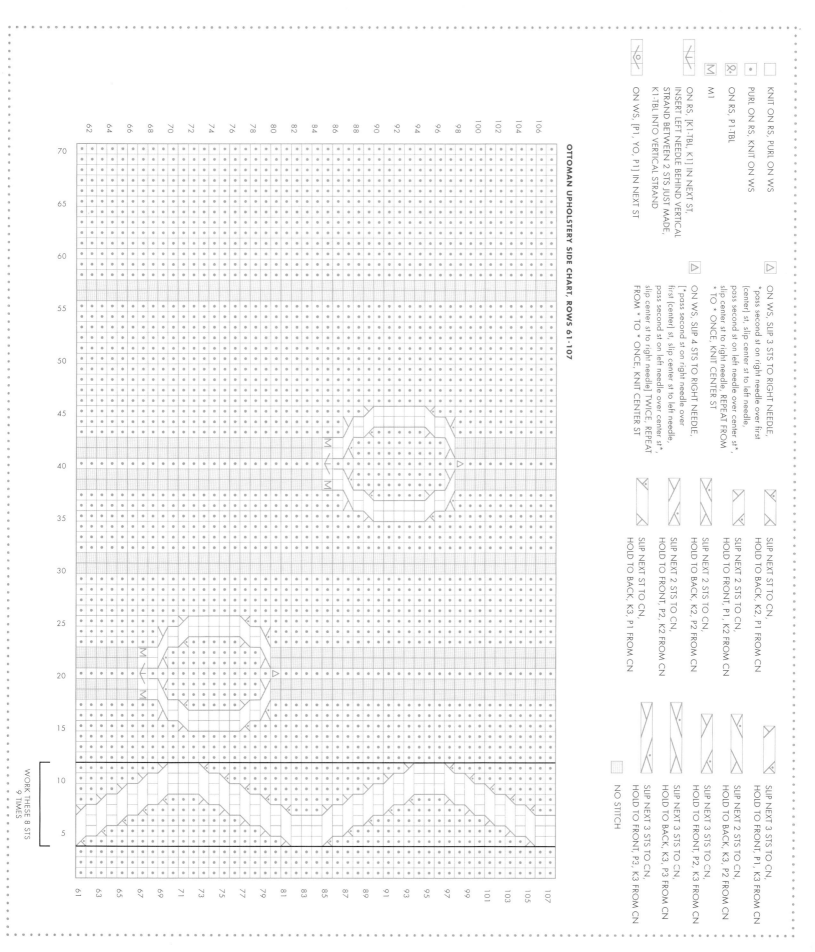

OTTOMAN UPHOLSTERY SIDE CHART, ROWS 61-107

WORK THESE 8 STS 9 TIMES

Legend:

☐ KNIT ON RS, PURL ON WS

• PURL ON RS, KNIT ON WS

ON RS, P1-TBL

M1

⊠ ON RS, [K1-TBL, K1] IN NEXT ST, INSERT LEFT NEEDLE BEHIND VERTICAL STRAND BETWEEN 2 STS JUST MADE, K1-TBL INTO VERTICAL STRAND

ON WS, [P1, YO, P1] IN NEXT ST

▷ ON WS, SLIP 3 STS TO RIGHT NEEDLE, *pass second st on right needle over first (center) st, slip center st to left needle, pass second st on left needle over center st*, slip center st to right needle, REPEAT FROM * TO * ONCE, KNIT CENTER ST

▷ ON WS, SLIP 4 STS TO RIGHT NEEDLE, [*pass second st on right needle over first (center) st, slip center st to left needle, pass second st on left needle over center st*, slip center st to right needle, REPEAT FROM * TO * ONCE, KNIT CENTER ST

SLIP NEXT ST TO CN, HOLD TO BACK, K2, P1 FROM CN

SLIP NEXT ST TO CN, HOLD TO FRONT, P1, K3 FROM CN

SLIP NEXT 2 STS TO CN, HOLD TO BACK, K3, P2 FROM CN

SLIP NEXT 2 STS TO CN, HOLD TO FRONT, P1, K2 FROM CN

SLIP NEXT 2 STS TO CN, HOLD TO BACK, K2, P2 FROM CN

SLIP NEXT 2 STS TO CN, HOLD TO FRONT, P2, K2 FROM CN

SLIP NEXT 2 STS TO CN, HOLD TO BACK, K3, P2 FROM CN

SLIP NEXT 3 STS TO CN, HOLD TO FRONT, P2, K3 FROM CN

SLIP NEXT 3 STS TO CN, HOLD TO BACK, K3, P3 FROM CN

SLIP NEXT 3 STS TO CN, HOLD TO FRONT, P3, K3 FROM CN

NO STITCH

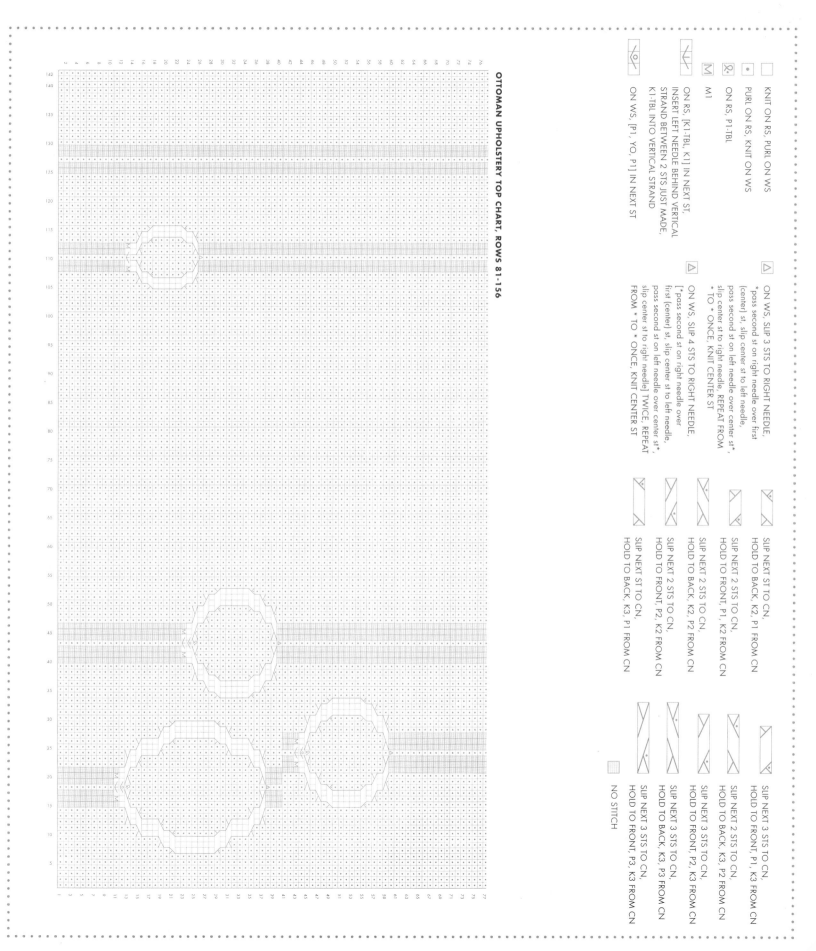

OTTOMAN UPHOLSTERY TOP CHART, ROWS 81-156

KNIT ON RS, PURL ON WS

PURL ON RS, KNIT ON WS

ON RS, P1-TBL

M1

ON RS, [K1-TBL, K1] IN NEXT ST, INSERT LEFT NEEDLE BEHIND VERTICAL STRAND BETWEEN 2 STS JUST MADE, K1-TBL INTO VERTICAL STRAND

ON WS, [P1, YO, P1] IN NEXT ST

ON WS, SLIP 3 STS TO RIGHT NEEDLE, *pass second st on right needle over first (center) st, slip center st to left needle, pass second st on left needle over center st*, slip center st to right needle, REPEAT FROM * TO * ONCE, KNIT CENTER ST

ON WS, SLIP 4 STS TO RIGHT NEEDLE, [*pass second st on right needle over first (center) st, slip center st to left needle, pass second st on left needle over center st*, slip center st to right needle] TWICE, REPEAT FROM * TO * ONCE, KNIT CENTER ST

SLIP NEXT ST TO CN, HOLD TO BACK, K2, P1 FROM CN

SLIP NEXT 2 STS TO CN, HOLD TO FRONT, P1, K3 FROM CN

SLIP NEXT 2 STS TO CN, HOLD TO BACK, K2, P2 FROM CN

SLIP NEXT 2 STS TO CN, HOLD TO FRONT, P1, K2 FROM CN

SLIP NEXT 2 STS TO CN, HOLD TO BACK, K3, P2 FROM CN

SLIP NEXT 3 STS TO CN, HOLD TO FRONT, P2, K3 FROM CN

SLIP NEXT 2 STS TO CN, HOLD TO BACK, K2, P2 FROM CN

SLIP NEXT 3 STS TO CN, HOLD TO FRONT, P2, K2 FROM CN

SLIP NEXT 3 STS TO CN, HOLD TO BACK, K3, P3 FROM CN

SLIP NEXT 3 STS TO CN, HOLD TO FRONT, P3, K3 FROM CN

NO STITCH

work even [...] worked a WS row. Change
to smaller needles and work
buttonholes as follows:

Row1 (RS): *K8, BO4, repeat from*
Row 2 (WS): *P8, CO4, repeat from*

Work 2 more rows of St. St. Change
to B and work 2 rows garter
St. BO all Sts.

appendix

embroidery motif

Take a look →

alternate type
of stitch
used

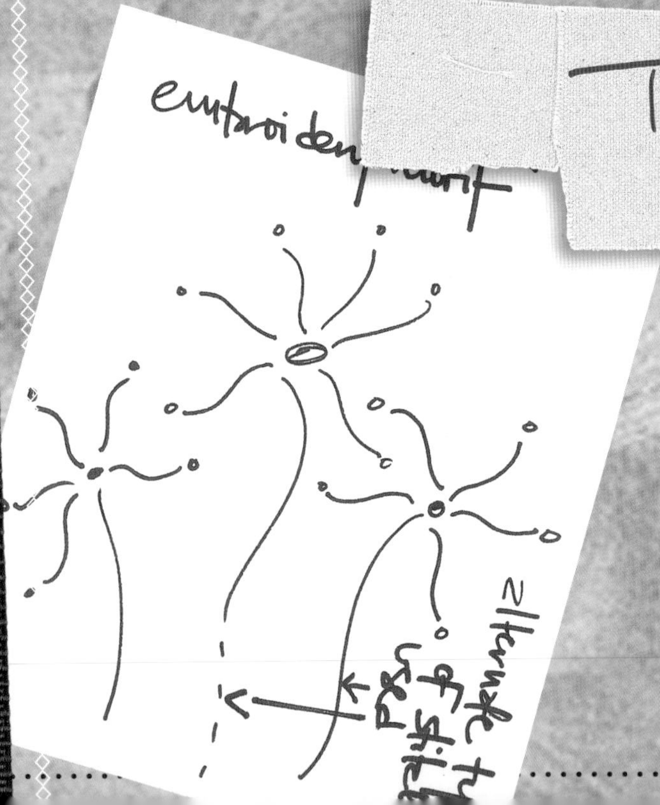

special techniques

BASTING: Work a running st, using long, loose sts.

BLANKET STITCH: Insert threaded needle into fabric about ¼" from fabric edge, and pull through. *Move over approximately ¼" and reinsert needle, bringing yarn under needle before pulling through. Repeat from * along fabric edge.

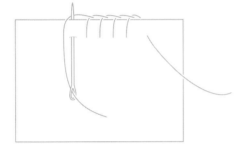

BLANKET STITCH

CROCHET CHAIN: Make a slip knot and place it on crochet hook. Holding tail end of yarn in left hand, *take hook under ball end of yarn from front to back; draw yarn on hook back through previous st on hook to form new st. Repeat from * to desired number of sts or length of chain.

FRENCH KNOT: Bring threaded needle up from WS of fabric to RS. Wrap yarn tautly around needle several times. Bring needle to WS, reinserting in fabric very close to but not in prior exit point. Pull yarn taut, forming knot on RS.

FRENCH KNOT

GARTER STITCH: Knit every row when working straight; knit 1 round, purl 1 round when working circular.

I-CORD: Using a double-pointed needle, cast on or pick up the required number of sts; the working yarn will be at the left end of the needle. *Hold the needle with the sts in your left hand, slide the sts to the right end of the needle, and bring the yarn around behind the work. Using a second double-pointed needle, knit the sts from right to left, pulling the yarn from left to right for the first st; do not turn. Repeat from * until the I-cord is the desired length. *Note: After a few rows, the tubular shape will become apparent.*

INTARSIA: Use a separate length of yarn for each color section. When changing colors, bring the new yarn up and to the right of the yarn just used to twist the yarns and prevent leaving a hole; do not carry colors not in use across the back of the work.

INVISIBLE STITCH: Place two pieces of fabric to be sewn together next to one another. Bring threaded needle out through fold at edge of first piece, and catch a tiny bit of the second piece. *Bring needle into fold, move tip of needle over 1/16 or 1/8" within fold, then bring needle out through fold. Catch a tiny bit of the second piece. Pull needle through, and repeat from *.

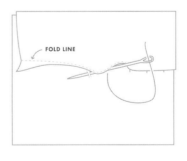

FOLD LINE

INVISIBLE STITCH

When working invisible stitch to sew a zipper into a felted item, work sts 1/16 or 1/8" from edge of felted fabric and zipper teeth.

MATTRESS STITCH: Lay two pieces of fabric side by side, with RS facing up. *Bring threaded needle under 2 strands of yarn near edge of first piece of fabric. Bring needle under 2 corresponding strands of yarn on second piece of fabric. Repeat from *, reinserting needle into a piece of fabric at the point from which the needle last exited the fabric.

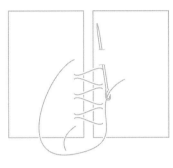

MATTRESS STITCH

READING CHARTS: Charts are read from right to left for RS rows, and from left to right for WS rows. Row numbers on the right indicate RS rows, and row numbers on the left indicate WS rows. The color or symbol within a square tells you how to work a st. Squares containing "no stitch" symbols are an exception: they do not correspond to stitches on your needles, but instead serve as "placeholders" within a chart, showing where sts have not yet been created through increasing or have been eliminated through decreasing. See also Intarsia, for working charts composed of blocks of color.

REVERSE STOCKINETTE STITCH *(Rev St st):* Purl on RS rows, knit on WS rows when working straight; purl every round when working circular.

RUNNING STITCH: *Insert threaded needle from RS of fabric to WS and back to RS a few times, then pull through. Repeat from *.

RUNNING STITCH

SATIN STITCH: Cover an area with closely spaced straight sts as follows: Bring threaded needle from WS to RS of fabric at one edge of area to be covered. *At opposite edge of area, bring needle from

RS to WS and back to RS, catching the smallest possible bit of the background fabric. Repeat from *, carefully tensioning the sts so the work lies flat without puckering.

SATIN STITCH

SHORT-ROW SHAPING: Work the number of sts specified in the instructions, then wrap and turn (wrp-t) as follows:
Bring yarn to the front, slip the next st to the right-hand needle, bring yarn to the back, return slipped st to left-hand needle; turn, ready to work the next row, leaving remaining sts unworked. When short rows are completed, or when working progressively longer short rows, work each wrap together with the st it wraps as follows: If st is to be knit, insert the right-hand needle into the wrap from below, then into the wrapped st, then knit them together. If st to be purled, lift back of wrap onto the left-hand needle, then purl together with the wrapped st.

STEM STITCH: Bring threaded needle from WS to RS of fabric. *Bring needle to WS to the right of the point at which the needle last exited the fabric, then bring needle to RS between those two points. Repeat from *, creating a series of sts that overlap slightly, each with a slight diagonal slant.

STEM STITCH

STOCKINETTE STITCH *(St st):* Knit on RS rows, purl on WS rows when working straight; knit every round when working circular.

WHIP STITCH: *Bring threaded needle from back to front through edges of both pieces of fabric, catching only as much fabric as necessary to create a firm seam. Bring needle over fabric edges and repeat from *, spacing sts close together.

abbreviations

BO: Bind off.

CC: Contrast color.

CN: Cable needle.

CO: Cast on.

dpn(s): Double-pointed needle(s).

k: Knit.

k1-f/b: Knit into front loop and back loop of next st to increase one st.

k2tog: Knit 2 sts together.

M1 (make 1): With the tip of the left-hand needle inserted from front to back, lift the strand between the two needles onto the left-hand needle; knit the strand through the back loop to increase one st.

MC: Main color.

p: Purl.

p2tog: Purl 2 sts together.

pm: Place marker.

psso: Pass slipped st over.

Rev St st: Reverse Stockinette st.

rnd(s): Round(s).

RS: Right side.

sl1-k1-psso: Slip a st as if to knit, knit a st, pass slipped st over knit st.

ssk (slip, slip, knit): Slip the next 2 sts to the right-hand needle one at a time as if to knit; return them back to the left-hand needle one at a time in their new orientation; knit them together through their back loops.

St st: Stockinette stitch.

st(s): Stitch(es).

tbl: Through back loop.

wrp-t: Wrap and turn (see Short-Row Shaping in Special Techniques, facing page).

WS: Wrong side.

yo: Yarnover.

sources for supplies

Beads
DAVA BEAD AND TRADE
1815 NE Broadway
Portland, OR 97232
877-962-3282
www.davabeadandtrade.com

Blocking Wires
HANDWORKS NORTHWEST
P.O. Box 19322
Portland, OR 97219
www.handworksnw.com

Buttons, Ribbon
BUTTON EMPORIUM
914 SW 11th Avenue
Portland, OR 97205
503-228-6372
www.buttonemporium.com

Fabric
BOLT NEIGHBORHOOD FABRIC BOUTIQUE
2136 NE Alberta Street
Portland, OR 97211
503-287-BOLT (2658)
www.boltfabricboutique.com

JOSEPHINE'S DRY GOODS
521 SW 11th Avenue
Portland, OR 97205
503-224-4202
www.josephinesdrygoods.com

FABRIC DEPOT
700 SE 122nd Avenue
Portland, OR 97233
888-896-1478
www.fabricdepot.com

THE WHOLE 9 YARDS
1820 East Burnside Street
Portland, OR 97214
503-223-2880
www.w9yards.com

Felting Supplies
Felting supplies can also be found at your local yarn and fabric stores
FINE FIBER PRESS & STUDIO (FELTING NEEDLES AND FOAM BLOCKS)
604 First Avenue East
Albany, OR 97321
541-917-3251
www.finefiberpress.com

WONDER WASHER (PORTABLE WASHING MACHINE)
item #26967
www.carolwrightgifts.com

WOOL MIX (FLEECE)
www.leighradford.com

Furniture
IKEA (OTTOMAN & CHAIRS)
www.ikea.com

Fusible Web
THE WARM COMPANY (STEAM-A-SEAM 2)
5529 186th Place SW
Lynnwood, WA 98037
800-234-WARM (9276)
www.warmcompany.com

Knitting Needles
LANTERN MOON
(wholesale only; contact or check website to locate a retailer near you)
800-530-4170
www.lanternmoon.com

Leather Bag Handles
HOMESTEAD HEIRLOOMS
N28W29868 Oakwood Grove Road
Pewaukee, WI 53072
262-352-8738
www.homesteadheirlooms.com

Printing & Copy Services
FEDEX KINKO'S
(large format copies)
800-254-6567
www.fedex.com

Recycled Wool
ANDY & BAX (ARMY BLANKETS)
324 SE Grand Avenue
Portland, OR 97214
503-234-7538
www.andyandbax.com

GOODWILL INDUSTRIES
(BLANKETS AND SWEATERS)
301-530-6500
www.goodwill.org

Rubber Bands
SCUNCI HAIR ELASTICS
Sold in the hair accessory
aisle of most drug stores.

BRAID BINDERS
Sold in tack shops and at
www.doversaddlery.com.

Yarn
BERROCO, INC.
14 Elmdale Road
P.O. Box 367
Uxbridge, MA 01569
508-278-2527
www.berroco.com

BLUE SKY ALPACAS
P.O. Box 88
Cedar, MN 55011
888-460-8862
www.blueskyalpacas.com

BROWN SHEEP COMPANY
100662 County Road 16
Mitchell, NE 69357
800-826-9136
www.brownsheep.com

FAIRMOUNT FIBERS
(MANOS DEL URUGUAY)
915 North 28th Street
Philadelphia, PA 19130
888-566-9970
www.fairmountfibers.com

HARRISVILLE DESIGNS
P.O. Box 806
Harrisville, NH 03450
800-338-9415
www.harrisvilledesigns.com

LOUET NORTH AMERICA
808 Commerce Park Dr.
Ogdensburg, NY 13669
613-925-4502
www.louet.com

MALABRIGO YARN
Haiti 1500
Montevideo 12800
Uruguay
786-866-6187 (US)
www.malabrigoyarn.com

MISTI INTERNATIONAL
ALPACA YARNS
P.O. Box 2532
Glen Ellyn, IL 60138
888-776-YARN (9276)
www.mistialpaca.com

MOREHOUSE FARM
141 Milan Hill Road
Red Hook, NY 12571
www.morehousefarm.com

PEAR TREE YARN
P.O. Box 463
Torquay, Victoria 3228
Australia
www.peartreeyarn.com

VERMONT ORGANIC FIBER
COMPANY
52 Seymour Street, Suite 8
Middlebury, VT 05753
802-388-1313
www.o-wool.com

WESTMINSTER FIBERS
(ROWAN YARNS)
165 Ledge Street
Nashua, NH 03060
800-445-9276
www.westminsterfibers.com

Other
SAINT CUPCAKE
407 NW 17th Avenue
Portland, OR 97209
503-473-8760
www.saintcupcake.com

SEAPLANE
827 NW 23rd Avenue
Portland, OR 97210
503-234-2409
www.e-seaplane.com

All clothing listed below from Seaplane.
Pages 38 & 40: Frocky Jack Morgan
   Party Dress
Page 64: Wool dress by Claire LaFaye
Page 76: Dress by Claire LaFaye;
   earrings by Amy Tavern

bibliography

BUDD, ANN
The Knitter's Handy Book of Sweater Patterns,
Interweave Press, 2004.

EVERS, INGE
Feltmaking: Techniques and Projects,
Lark Books, 1987.

GALESKAS, BEVERLY
Felted Knits,
Interweave Press, 2003.

HIATT, JUNE HEMMONS
The Principles of Knitting: Methods and Techniques of Hand Knitting,
Simon & Schuster, 1988.

SJOBERG, GUNILLA PAETAU
Felt: New Directions for an Ancient Craft,
Interweave Press, 1996.

STANLEY, MONTSE
Reader's Digest Knitter's Handbook,
Reader's Digest, 1993.

WADA, YOSHIKO IWAMOTO
Memory on Cloth: Shibori Now,
Kodansha International, 2002.

WORLD SHIBORI NETWORK
shibori.org

acknowledgments

— • —

No one ever creates a book alone. I AM SO GRATEFUL TO THE TALENTED GROUP OF PEOPLE WHO CONTRIBUTED THEIR TIME AND TALENTS TO THIS ONE: TO Melanie Falick, MY EDITOR, WHOSE CONFIDENCE IN ME AND STEADY ENCOURAGEMENT INSPIRE ME TO DO MY BEST WORK; TO John Mulligan, WHOSE BEAUTIFUL PHOTOGRAPHY FILLS THESE PAGES; TO MODELS Carma Ferrier, Kacy Owens, Nito AND Elijah Taufui, Wendy Swartz, AND Kate Towers, WHO MAKE THE PROJECTS LOOK SO GOOD; TO Claudine Ebel, FOR EXPERT HAIR AND MAKEUP; TO Jenny AT ALLEN'S TREE FARM, Karen Ford AND John Dingler, Julie AND Satoru Igarashi, Kate Towers AND Holly Stadler AT SEAPLANE, AND Suzi Johnson AT SOUCHI FOR GRACIOUSLY WELCOMING US INTO THEIR HOMES AND BUSINESSES FOR PHOTOGRAPHY.

SPECIAL THANKS TO THE MULTITALENTED Laura Irwin—YOUR ASSISTANCE, TALENT, ORGANIZATION, AND GOOD SENSE OF HUMOR WERE INVALUABLE—AND TO Cindy Taylor, FOR ENCOURAGEMENT AND VERY WISE WORDS AND FOR HAVING A CUPCAKE FROM SAINT CUPCAKE DELIVERED TO MY DOOR ON A DAY WHEN I REALLY NEEDED SOME ICING!

THANKS TO KNITTERS Anne Berk, Adriano Gonzalez, Laura Irwin, Patricia Harrington, AND Hilary Holiday, WHOSE PRODUCTION ASSISTANCE WAS INVALUABLE! THANKS ALSO TO THE TEAM AT LANTERN MOON, ESPECIALLY Joel Woodcock, Sharon Woodcock, AND Bruce Feller, WHOSE PATIENCE ALLOWED ME TO FOCUS ON COMPLETING THIS BOOK. THANKS TO JC Briar FOR MAKING THE TECHNICAL-EDITING PROCESS LESS STRESSFUL AND TO Kat, Diane, AND Jennifer AT Goodesign, WHO ONCE AGAIN HAVE DESIGNED SUCH A BEAUTIFUL BOOK!

I MUST ALSO THANK THE FOLLOWING YARN COMPANIES WHO SO GENEROUSLY PROVIDED YARN FOR THE PROJECTS: Berroco, Blue Sky Alpacas, Brown Sheep Company, Fairmount Fibers, Harrisville Designs, Louet North America, Malabrigo Yarn, Misti International Alpaca Yarns, Morehouse Farm, Pear Tree Yarn, Vermont Organic Fiber Company, AND Westminster Fibers.

SPECIAL THANKS TO MY FAMILY, Matt, Cass, AND Carol, AND FRIENDS Elaine AND George Chambers, Laura Irwin, Linda Lee, Marybeth Lynn, Sue Stahl, AND Dawn Witherspoon—YOUR ONGOING SUPPORT AND ENCOURAGEMENT MAKE IT POSSIBLE FOR ME TO STAY ON MY CREATIVE PATH.

about the author

Leigh Radford IS AN AWARD-WINING AUTHOR, DESIGNER, AND TEACHER WHO FREQUENTLY EXPLORES IMAGINATIVE APPLICATIONS OF TRADITIONAL AND NONTRADITIONAL MATERIALS. SHE IS THE AUTHOR OF AlterKnits: Imaginative Projects and Creativity Exercises (STEWART, TABORI & CHANG) AND One Skein: 30 Quick Projects to Knit and Crochet, AND IS THE CREATOR OF Silk Gelato, A SILK RIBBON YARN DISTRIBUTED BY Lantern Moon. IN WORKSHOPS AROUND THE COUNTRY, Leigh ENCOURAGES STUDENTS TO CHALLENGE THE RULES OF CONVENTION AS THEY EXPLORE THE REALM OF THE IMAGINATION. ALWAYS LOOKING FOR WAYS TO STRETCH HER DESIGN BOUNDARIES, SHE IS CURRENTLY WORKING ON HER BFA AT OREGON COLLEGE OF ARTS AND CRAFTS. TO SEE MORE OF HER WORK, VISIT LEIGHRADFORD.COM.